THE RHETORIC OF
MODERN STATESMANSHIP

The Rhetoric of Modern Statesmanship

Volume 18

Exxon Education Foundation Series on Rhetoric and Political Discourse

Edited by

Kenneth W. Thompson

Miller Center of Public Affairs
University of Virginia

University Press of America

Lanham • New York • London

The Miller Center

University of Virginia

Copyright © 1992 by
University Press of America®, Inc.
4720 Boston Way
Lanham, Maryland 20706

3 Henrietta Street
London WC2E 8LU England

Co-published by arrangement with
The Miller Center of Public Affairs,
University of Virginia

The views expressed by the author(s) of this publication do not necessarily
represent the opinions of the Miller Center. We hold to Jefferson's dictum that:
"Truth is the proper and sufficient antagonist to error, and has nothing to
fear from the conflict, unless by human interposition, disarmed of her
natural weapons, free argument and debate."

Library of Congress Cataloging-in-Publication Data

Thompson, Kenneth W., 1921–
The rhetoric of modern statesmanship / [edited by
Kenneth W. Thompson].
p.   cm. — (Exxon Education Foundation series on
rhetoric and political discourse ; v. 18)
1. Political oratory.   2. Rhetoric—Political aspects.
3. Statesmen—Language.   4. World politics—1975–1985.
5. World politics—1985–1995.   I. Series.
PN4193.P6T48   1992   808.5'1'08835—dc20   91–40788 CIP

ISBN 0–8191–8519–1 (cloth : alk. paper)
ISBN 0–8191–8520–5 (pbk. : alk. paper)

 The paper used in this publication meets the minimum requirements of
American National Standard for Information Sciences—Permanence
of Paper for Printed Library Materials, ANSI Z39.48–1984.

To those who lead

through clarity and coherence

of

thought or expression

whether to

understand or legislate

Table of Contents

Preface

The preface of Volume I of the Miller Center series on rhetoric begins:

> For the Miller Center as for most institutes of public affairs or communications, the subject of rhetoric and discourse looms large. In an era in which the popularity of the nation's chief executive rests substantially on his skills as a communicator, the topic of rhetoric has found its way back into the center of the political vocabulary. Not by accident, America's most popular president since Kennedy, or perhaps since Eisenhower, if not Franklin D. Roosevelt, will be remembered as "the great communicator."

We went on to say:

> The aim of this series of lectures is to rediscover the classical meaning of rhetoric, to study the forces that undermined it and brought about a change and to consider how and why it came to be associated with a falsifying strategy of language and ethics.

As we come to the end of the rhetoric series, we continue to ask what is the place of rhetoric in society and statesmanship in the late 20th century. What lessons can we draw from the past? What is unique about rhetoric in the late 20th century?

In the Miller Center's inquiry we have pursued in 19 previous volumes, first, the historical and philosophical background of the rhetoric of modern statesmanship with some of the world's most profound thinkers. We next considered the most persistent problems of contemporary rhetoric in modern statesmanship as illustrated in presidential speechmaking and the political rhetoric of leaders and presidents. Following that, we examined the rhetoric of individual statesmen in contemporary societies. Finally, we examined the rhetoric and policies of statesmen as they confronted urgent problems.

This final volume on rhetoric and modern statesmanship seeks to summarize and integrate the lessons from earlier papers in the series. It is intended both as a synthesis and an updating of the substance of what has gone before. It brings to a point of focus rhetoric and contemporary statesmanship and the principles that derive from the history and philosophy of rhetoric. Statesmanship involves both the essence and the application of rhetoric. For the present series, it represents the culmination of an inquiry that has occupied the Miller Center since 1986, or the better part of half a decade. Statesmanship is rhetoric in action and the dynamics of communications in the arenas of power. For the late 20th century, it matters no less and in fact more than it did in the ancient polity.

Introduction

A first step in understanding the place of rhetoric in modern statesmanship is the examination of the institutions in whose name statesmen speak. No observer of the modern state system and the United States in particular had a clearer grasp of political realities than the Frenchman Alexis de Tocqueville. The first essay in the present volume deals with Tocqueville, democracy, and the moral issue in American statecraft. Its author is a young scholar who is already an acknowledged authority on the concept of the national interest. He is Professor W. David Clinton III of Tulane University. Clinton is the author of a forthcoming study of the national interest that promises to carry further the discussion initiated by writers such as Hans J. Morgenthau and Charles Beard. Clinton's paper is an elegant analysis of Tocqueville's approach to democracy and the nation state. It places in historical context the consideration of rhetoric and modern statesmanship. It reminds us that more than abstract moral principles are required. Morality and moral statements must be related to the national interests of sovereign states.

Ladd Hamilton is an old-fashioned journalist with an old-fashioned view of rhetoric. Hamilton had the temerity to ask in a column in the *New York Times* whether our lack of knowledge of our political leaders is a result of their dependence on speechwriters. How can we judge a political leader when his words are not his own, Hamilton asks. How do we know his real thoughts and convictions? For Hamilton, language defines the speaker. The words in the surrender speech of an Indian chief, he tells us, were not only Joseph's. They *were* Joseph.

Robert Orben is a presidential speech writer and a humorist. His approach offers an opposing view of what political leaders must do and say. Having written for Red Skelton and for after-dinner speeches by business executives, he has a different conception of what the public requires. Ladd Hamilton's and Robert Orben's presentations read side by side provide two dimensions of political speeches that are current in American political life.

Gaddis Smith is one of a handful of American diplomatic historians who tower above colleagues just as his mentor, Samuel Flagg Bemis, was preeminent among earlier American diplomatic historians. He seeks to understand presidential rhetoric by analyzing the public rhetoric of President Jimmy Carter and holding it up for evaluation in terms of the standards set forth in the book *Modern Rhetoric*. Those standards are *argument, exposition, description,* and *narration*. Thus Professor Smith seeks an objective basis for his analysis, and of the four standards, *argument* has primacy in political rhetoric. Professor Smith's strongest criticism of Carter's public communication is that "He spoke as if the audience for Jimmy Carter was Jimmy Carter." To understand that criticism, it is necessary to read Gaddis Smith's chapter in full.

Having examined the historical and philosophical background of modern statesmanship, we consider in Part III the rhetoric of certain contemporary statesmen. They are chosen because they stand out in what some argue is a speech writer-ridden form of contemporary rhetoric. That at least is the suggestion of the *New York Times* columnist Russell Baker in the first selection in Part Three.

The following two papers deal with the presidential rhetoric of two presidents who are generally considered the greatest of modern presidential communicators. Halford Ryan is a professor of rhetoric at Washington and Lee University and Tom Griscom was a staff assistant to Senator Howard Baker in the White House and the Senate. Their assessments of the two great communicators are important for what they explain and what yet remains a mystery concerning the skill and success of FDR and Reagan.

Perhaps the postwar foreign policy that had the greatest impact was the Marshall Plan. It led to the recovery of Western Europe. To this day, Americans confronted by great and insoluble problems are prone to say "we need a Marshall Plan"—whether for Latin America or the cities. It is not without consequence, therefore, that we know more about its origins, the planners who brought it about, and the speech in which it was first enunciated. Forrest C. Pogue is the Marshall historian and formerly director of the research program at the Marshall Library. In a rather lengthy and immensely scholarly review, Pogue traces the background of the speech at Harvard in which Secretary of State George Marshall announced the Marshall Plan. While this selection goes well beyond technical rhetorical analysis, it provides the more or less definitive explanation of the Marshall speech.

The final section of this volume deals with change in the world and discourse and relations among statesmen and nations. General George M. Seignious II offers reflections on the rhetoric and reality of change in the Soviet Union, a process that we continue to assess in an ongoing inquiry into a world in change.

Another area in which the rhetoric of discourse played a prominent role was the European Community. Most observers see Jean Monnet as the architect of the modern idea of a United Europe. His vision was an inspiration to other Europeans. Ambassador John W. Tuthill knew Monnet and offers a perspective on how he "managed to reason, cajole, argue, circumvent, and bully the reluctant European governments . . ." toward the creation of a Europe expected to reach a new measure of unity in 1992.

Finally, Russell Baker's reflections on presidential rhetoric, humor, and social criticism brings our long journey to an end. If "laughter is the beginning of prayer," humor may be the appropriate note on which to close an extended discourse on rhetoric.

I.

THE HISTORICAL AND PHILOSOPHICAL BACKGROUND

CHAPTER 1

Tocqueville, Democracy, and the Moral Issue in American Statecraft*

DAVID CLINTON

The name of Alexis de Tocqueville is not generally associated with the study of international relations. Social analyst, political thinker, and informed commentator on the fundamental intellectual currents of the age, he has left the illumination for posterity of the states-system in the first half of the 19th century to others, such as Lord Brougham, Friedrich von Gentz, Richard Cobden, Jeremy Bentham, and Tocqueville's own friend and interpreter, John Stuart Mill.[1] Yet while he was not primarily concerned with foreign affairs, he did not ignore them. Some of the most famous passages in his most famous book (at least in the United States), *Democracy in America*, point to the capacities, or incapacities, of democracies in conducting foreign policy. In his 1852 lecture to the Académie des Sciences Morales et Politiques as its president, he attempted to define the "science of politics,"

*Paper presented at the annual meeting of the Southwestern Science Association on 23-26 March 1988 in Houston, Texas.

in part by identifying its four constituent parts, one of which was the study of international law and the relations among states undertaken by Grotius and Pufendorf. His service in the Chamber of Deputies under the Orleanist Monarchy and the Second Republic from 1839 to 1851 brought him into contact with the foreign and colonial questions of the day; it was he who largely wrote the reports of two committees on which he served during those years, dealing with the abolition of slavery in France's West Indian possessions and French military and colonial policy in Algeria. The highest post—and sole Cabinet responsibility—he attained in this world of practical politics was that of foreign minister in 1849.

Tocqueville's views on international relations, as they can be discerned from his published writings and correspondence, may not be without interest, therefore, particularly because they deal on the level of the states-system with the vital problem that preoccupied him in all his work throughout his life: preserving liberty, diversity, and virtue in an epoch of increasing uniformity. Though scattered, his reflections on the subject form, by and large, a coherent whole that merits our renewed attention. In this paper I shall set out what I believe Tocqueville took to be a central normative concern in international relations. I shall then discuss his preferred courses of action in response to the dangers he saw in the international society of his day. Finally, the applicability of both his fears and his hopes to the foreign policy of the United States will be the subject of my conclusion.

The Progress of Equality: Inevitable but Troubling

"A great democratic revolution is taking place in our midst"—Tocqueville believed that this social change was the premier reality of the modern age. He began his analysis of American society by noting that nothing in the United States had struck him more vividly than "the equality of conditions" there and "the immense influence of this basic fact on the whole course of society," and he promised his readers that the universal influence of this equalizing trend would be the thread binding together all the particular incidents, institutions, and practices he described in the pages that followed.[2] In the Old World, meanwhile, he "saw an equality of conditions which, though it had not reached the extreme limits found in the United States, was daily drawing closer, thereto"; he asserted that "that same democracy which prevailed over the societies of America seemed to me to be advancing rapidly toward power in Europe." If this revolution was geographically widespread, it was also long-lived: in the introduction to *Democracy in America*, the author traced its origins back for at least seven centuries. He captured in *The Ancien Regime and the Revolution* one of its most dramatic episodes in the history of his own country, and intended to continue the story in a sequel volume for which only the notes were left at his death.

The progress of equality had broken down all hierarchies and traditional distinctions among classes and estates. Political, military, economic, religious, and technological changes had all tended in the direction of rendering illegitimate and then obliterating differences of all kinds, "throughout the Christian world." "Democracy," then, meant levelling, effacing whatever privileges or customs served to distinguish one person from another. This democracy might be accomplished in equal liberty or in equal servitude, but its progressive attainment seemed an "irresistible revolution advancing century by century over every obstacle." Those, like Tocqueville himself, primarily concerned with the fostering of liberty might hope to guide the democratic juggernaut in ways that would avoid the despotic form of equality, but they could not expect, even if they wished, to halt or reverse it.

It was this inexorable, seemingly illimitable, quality to the democratic revolution that brought to the fore Tocqueville's concerns in the international realm. Taken to its logical conclusion, the erasing of all distinctions among individuals would overwhelm the boundaries among states. Having overcome the barriers of class, of wealth, of religion, of region, the movement toward equality of condition seemed unlikely to be stopped by the barrier of citizenship. Rather, as it approached fulfillment within states with increasing rapidity and force, it would begin—had already begun—to undermine the distinctions among states and the legitimacy of treating citizens or nationals differently from other human beings. Every previous attempt to set bounds to the democratic revolution had been defeated; every previous prediction that it had reached its natural limits had been falsified. "Will it stop now," Tocqueville asked, "when it has grown so strong and its adversaries so weak?"

The destruction of distinctive national traditions was a product of the progress of a similar conception of reason, which overcame national traits and characteristics of thought. While in the United States, Tocqueville made the point in his notebook:

> If ever the world comes to be completely civilized, the human race will in appearance form only one people. Reason, like virtue, does not bend at all in different climates, and does not vary with temperaments and the nature of places. It is one, it is inflexible. Everywhere it tends to the same end, and progresses by the same roads. All the peoples, then, that take reason for the guide of their actions must have great points of resemblance: to think, to believe, to feel the same things in a whole [range] of circumstances.[3]

Twelve years later, he noted that the influence of religion tended in the same direction: "Christianity and consequently its morality went beyond all political powers and nationalities. Its grand achievement is to have formed a human community beyond national societies."[4] From this point, the step is easily made to the position that moral obligations exist among all persons, as persons, and differences of nationality or the interests of state are not a legitimate moral consideration.[5]

Tocqueville, however, did not wish to take the step, because he did not favor the destruction of the national barrier to complete equality of conditions. "I am convinced," he wrote in a manuscript left unfinished at his death, "that the interests of the human race are better served by giving every man a particular fatherland than by trying to inflame his passions for the whole of humanity."[6] He led up to this conclusion in a reflection on the value—for the national society, but ultimately for the rest of humanity as well—of patriotism:

> From a general, higher viewpoint patriotism, despite its great impulses and deeds, would seem a false and narrow passion. The great efforts suggested by patriotism are in reality due to humanity, and not to those small fragments of the human race within particular limits called peoples or nations. It would seem, at first sight, that those Christian moralists especially who are inclined to care more for humanity than for their fatherland are right. Yet this is but a detour, at the end of which we will find that they are wrong.
>
> Man has been created by God (I do not know why) in such a way that the larger the object of his love the less directly attached he is to it. His heart needs particular passions; he needs limited objects for his affections to keep these firm and enduring. There are but few who will burn with ardent love for the entire human species. For the most part, the sole means by which Providence (man taken as he is) lets each of us work for the general good of humanity is to divide this great object into many smaller parts, making each of these fragments a worthy object of love to those who compose it. If everyone fulfills his duties in that way (and within

these limits such duties are not beyond anyone's natural capacities if properly directed by morals and reason), the general good of humanity would be produced by the many, despite the absence of more direct efforts except by a few.

Public spirit and civic virtue could be kept alive in the minds of most citizens only when the object of their patriotism was close enough to see, to understand, and to influence. In his discussion of American federalism, Tocqueville pointed to the strength enjoyed by the states of the Union, which "enfolded every citizen and in one way or another affected every detail of daily life." "State sovereignty is supported by memories, customs, local prejudices, and provincial and family selfishness; in a word," he noted, "it is supported by all those things which make the instinct of patriotism so powerful in the hearts of men." With the focus of their loyalty close at hand, citizens would most easily see the necessity and the effectiveness of their taking part in its governance. They could be most easily persuaded to make the sacrifices to preserve free institutions if these institutions were accessible. But the more remote the governing authority, the less likely the citizen was to rouse himself to defend the public interest, and the more prone he was to devote himself to purely private pursuits. While erstwhile citizens looked after their families or gave themselves over to the acquisition of wealth and material comforts, the public good would go unattended and the decay of liberal democratic institutions would transform their citizens into subjects.

All extensive political units were subject to this danger, in Tocqueville's view. The American federal government was to most of its citizens only "a huge and distant motherland and a vague, ill-defined sentiment," which rested on the loyalties freely given to the states: "Public spirit in the Union is, in a sense, only a summing up of provincial patriotism." Any large country would face a considerable challenge in preserving public spirit: "All passions fatal to a republic grow with the increase of its territory, but the virtues which should support it do not grow at the same rate." But combatting the tendency toward short-sighted materialistic individualism in even the largest nation would be an easy task compared with the struggle to preserve public spirit in the sprawling supranational empire established when the march of the principle of equality toppled political institutions built on national differences. Deadening uniformity of the kind Tocqueville associated with Eastern despotisms would only be made worse by the fact that the submergence of the prior states-system would leave no place in which dissidents could seek asylum and refuge.

The Society of States

Although Tocqueville did not believe the advance of democracy could be halted, he did think its path could be altered. In particular, humanity still had a choice between equality combined with freedom and equality that suffocated freedom. While equality would triumph as man's natural condition, it could be modified by artificial means that preserved useful supports to liberty; Tocqueville's writings are filled with examples of such works of artifice: federalism, administrative decentralization, the jury system and other legal forms, and, most important, the art of associating together, outside the framework of government, for shared ends. (Religion, although it had different origins, shared this instrumental character.) On the broadest level, this list of freedom-promoting expedients included the sustaining of a system of independent states as foci for the loyalty and citizen virtue of their inhabitants.

The progress of equality within states would continue, a process that Tocqueville contended was further advanced in Europe than most of his contemporaries understood. Indeed, if liberty were to survive in these states—in Tocqueville's terms, if they were to become democratic republics rather democratic despotisms—the advance of equality would necessarily be roughly simultaneous in all these states. If it were not, the free democracies, or democratic republics, which he expected to be unskillful at conducting foreign policy, would probably fall prey to their less free but more adept neighbors:

> For a democratic republic to survive without trouble in a European nation, it would be necessary for republics to be established in all the others at the same time. . . . If for a century a democratic country were to remain under a republican government, one can believe that at the end of that time it would be richer, more populated, and more prosperous than neighboring despotic states; but during that century it would often have run the risk of being conquered by them.[7]

But this equality would not progress so far as to erase the differences in laws and mores among states, or to endanger their sovereignty.

Preservation of the state required, in addition to the institutional devices noted above, a renewed attention to patriotism. Tocqueville was firmly of the opinion that religious teaching should inculcate civic virtue, even while it avoided party politics:

> I do not ask the clergy to make those whom it educates, or influences, conscientiously Republicans or Royalists. But I wish it to tell them more frequently, that while Christians, they also belong to one of the great Human Societies which God has formed, apparently in order to show more clearly the ties by which individuals ought to be mutually attached—societies which are called nations, inhabiting a territory, which they call their country. I wish the clergy to instil into their very

> souls that every one belongs much more to this collective Being than he does to himself; that towards this Being no one ought to be indifferent, much less, by treating such indifference as a sort of languid virtue, to enervate many of our noblest instincts; that every one is responsible for the fortunes of this collective Being; that every one is bound to work out its prosperity, and to watch that it be not governed except by respectable, beneficent, and legitimate authorities.[8]

Such teaching would be useless, however, unless states showed themselves to be worthy of the loyalty and sacrifices of their citizens. It was necessary in their foreign policy that states display a willingness to defend their interests and an ability to take what Tocqueville called "heroic" actions. No one of his day was more devoted to Anglo-French amity, but when in 1840 he believed that the British government had shown insufficient consideration for its partner's interests, he was quick to call for a stiff French retort and to criticize the government in Paris for what he saw as undue meekness in the face of provocation. His attitude during the crisis was primarily due to the impact he feared it might have on public opinion; as he explained in a letter to John Stuart Mill, "if it be important to keep up in a nation, especially in a nation so versatile as ours, the feeling that leads to great actions, the people must not be taught to submit quietly to be treated with indifference." The July Monarchy could not afford to dampen whatever ardor it aroused among its people: "To show no sense of your treatment of us would have been to smother, and perhaps extinguish, passions which we may some day need. The most elevated feeling now left to us is national pride. No doubt we ought to try to regulate it, and to moderate its ebullitions; but we must beware of diminishing it."[9]

Imperialism was an example of such a "heroic" action that, by arousing the imagination of the people, could capture their loyalty and inspire them to lift their eyes from their private pursuits and look to the common weal.[10] In 1830, as planning went forward for the first French expedition against Algiers, Tocqueville remarked in a letter to his brother that those previously skeptical about the venture, "since war has been resolved on, . . . have in general ceased to criticise both the end in view and the preparations." "The unanimity of opinion upon this point," he wrote approvingly, "shows the spirit of the nation."[11] Nor did he limit himself to French imperialism in his advocacy of any expansionist mission that he thought both civilized those in the conquered territory and elevated the thoughts of those in the conquering nation. At the time of the Mutiny of 1857, he urged a British correspondent that her country should remain in possession of India: "Nothing under the sun is so wonderful as the conquest, and still more the government, of India by the English. Nothing so fixes the eyes of mankind on the little island of which the Greeks never heard even the name." Even if, "as a mere question of money and of physical strength, India costs more than it brings in, . . . England obeys an instinct, not only heroic, but wise" in reasserting control to her greater glory.[12] Earlier, he had expressed a similar attitude toward British actions in China and the expansion of European influence in general.[13]

In all of this, we see how important Tocqueville believed it was for states to display vitality and the ability to act, even if, on some occasions, for no other reason than to demonstrate they *could* still act. At times, this action could result in war, and despite his conviction that war was hazardous to liberty because of the centralization of governmental authority it promoted and the popular acclaim it gave to military leaders who might turn themselves into military despots, he was prepared to acknowledge that at times it could contribute to civic virtue, that it had in fact "great advantages":

> I do not wish to speak ill of war; war almost always widens a nation's mental horizons and raises its heart. In some cases it may be the only factor which can prevent the exaggerated growth of certain inclinations naturally produced by equality and be the antidote needed for certain inveterate diseases to which democratic societies are liable.[14]

It has been argued that Tocqueville thought some degree of internal political turmoil was necessary to the health of a regime, because it jolted citizens out of their individual preoccupations and forced them to think of the best way to preserve their freedom. He seems to have believed that political turmoil, in the clash of proud nations and their heroic acts, was necessary in the states-system as well, to preserve the health of its component parts.[15]

If the parts are to be thus secured, what of the whole? In detailing the ways in which states could preserve themselves and avoid submergence in a featureless uniformity fatal to individual liberty and public spirit, it is easy to forget the increasing equality of condition and impatience with artificial distinctions among groups that caused Tocqueville to fear for the national community in the first place. We have seen that his basic assumption was that "the gradual progress of equality is something fated . . . universal and permanent."[16] How would it express itself in a political system run on the principle of the separate sovereignty of its members and marked by a distinct hierarchy running from the great powers to the small?

Tocqueville hoped the answer would be found in the very "reputation" that states would burnish by their self-assertion. Renown or glory could mean nothing unless there were common standards for judging who merited them and why they were praiseworthy. The international system would be best served if the pressure for egalitarianism could be channeled into a shared code of conduct that all European, or "civilized," states would consider themselves bound by. He was certainly convinced that this homogenization of Europe was already well advanced; he told Nassau Senior in a letter of 1852 that "in this great nation, called Europe, similar currents of opinions and feelings prevail, different as may be the institutions and characters of its different populations"—a contention he assumed needed no evidence beyond the general reaction against the revolutionary feeling (itself also continent-wide) of 1848.[17] He repeated the sentiment to his friend three years later, saying, "In the period in which we live, and, still more, in the period which is approaching, no European nation can long remain absolutely dissimilar to all the others."[18] His public rhetoric followed much the same line. In his speech to the Chamber of Deputies during the 1840 Anglo-French crisis, he spoke of "the general public good sense of Europe" and of the "moral necessity which European opinion" created. In the end, he claimed, if France stated its justifiable demands clearly and demonstrated that they were consonant with the European consensus, Britain would yield, because "a sort of universal reason rested on each government in particular and obliged it to conform to its judgments."[19]

In the end, the governments in both London and Paris did yield to the criticisms of Tocqueville and his colleagues in the events of 1840, making this an episode he could claim as evidence in support of the contention that international expectations influenced the actions of even powerful states. He accepted the wisdom of a certain modesty in calling others to account; "I acknowledge," he wrote to Reeve in March 1853, "that one is never in a position to judge of what appertains to the honour and interests of a foreign nation; that it alone is able to judge of these questions; that there is always some absurdity, in public or in private life, in giving advice to one's neighbors."[20] Nevertheless, he held that there were actions which any state that called itself civilized simply could not countenance, and it was the community or society of states bound by these common standards, and not the melding or superseding of those states by any broader unity, that, for him, was the desirable expression of equality in a democratic age.

If the norms of this society were to have any reality, they had to affect the policies of states, even when those states might find it expedient to act otherwise. In *Democracy in America*, Tocqueville had stressed the principle of self-interest rightly understood as a way, in an individualistic, nondeferential era, of linking individuals to their national community. In a somewhat similar fashion, he identified a number of ways in which states did, or could, make apparent sacrifices of their short-term interests to strengthen the international society that was the best guarantee of their own preservation and freedom in the long term.

The duties to the society of states that might require sacrifices from its members were several. One was a duty to secure a balance of power by preventing the preponderance of any one state. This might require states to act in defense of the system before their own interests were immediately threatened. In a letter to Senior written during the Crimean War, Tocqueville criticized the "detestable jealousies and ambitions of the European nations" that prevented them from cooperating against the greatest potential power, Russia.[21] Preserving adequate power against a potential threat could also require expanding the size of one's own country, and thereby courting the risk that free domestic institutions would be imperiled. In his analysis of the United States, Tocqueville granted that "in general terms . . . nothing is more inimical to human prosperity and freedom than great empires," but he insisted that this consideration might have to yield to the "necessity" imposed by the strength of adversaries:

> If there were only small nations and no large ones, humanity would most certainly be more free and happier; but there is no way of providing that there should not be large nations.
> The latter bring into the world a new element of national prosperity, that is, force. What does

> comfort or freedom profit a nation if it is in daily danger of being ravaged or conquered? What good are its industries and trade if another rules the seas and lays down the law in all markets? Small nations are often wretched not because they are small but because they are weak; the great ones prosper not because they are large but because they are strong. Therefore force is often for nations one of the primary conditions of happiness and even of existence. As a result of this, except in peculiar circumstances, small nations always end up by being forcibly united with great ones or by combining among themselves. I know nothing more deplorable than the state of a nation which can neither defend itself nor provide for itself.[22]

Playing a great, and necessary, role in the shifting conditions of the states-system demanded as well a tempering of democracy in the conduct of foreign affairs. Tocqueville's low opinion of the skill displayed by democratic states in their foreign relations was a life-long conviction, steadily maintained from a letter written at the outset of his career to his kinsman, Count Molé, asserting that "democracy, with an army of followers, has no generals," to his remembrances written in political retirement, in which he concluded that democracies, "as a rule, have only very confused and very erroneous ideas on external affairs . . . and generally solve foreign questions only by internal reasons."[23]

The balance of power rested on a rough consensus among the players on their rights, interests, and duties. Beyond this, there existed for Tocqueville a further obligation to lead this consensus in a liberal direction. The bedrock for such an enlightened general agreement lay in an understanding between Britain and France, the two liberal great powers after 1830—an understanding for which he pressed throughout his political life. "I believe the union of the two nations to be essential to the maintenance of free institutions in Europe," he wrote in 1836, "and in my opinion this consideration surpasses every other."[24] In her own actions, France was bound to set an example, not least by demonstrating that she was capable of making her imperialism high-minded. Thus, Tocqueville in a letter outlining his projected journey to Algiers, the first of two he was to make to France's most prized overseas possession: "The African question, complicated and important as it is, may be summed up in these words:—How shall we succeed in raising a French population, with our laws, our manners, and our civilisation, and at the same time treat the natives with the consideration to which we are bound by honour, by justice, by humanity, and by our real interest?"[25] This attitude would be reflected in the report Tocqueville helped to write the following year for a special parliamentary commission established to study the problem of colonization in Algeria.[26]

In his service as foreign minister from June through October of 1849, Tocqueville had the opportunity to try to put these sentiments into practice. One instance will be mentioned briefly here: French policy toward the occupation of Rome by revolutionary forces arising as a consequence of the revolutionary upheavals of 1848. It revealed Tocqueville's attitude as a liberal but not an egalitarian, a man prepared to wield power but not (he hoped) to abuse it.

When he became foreign minister at a time of great domestic and international ferment, Tocqueville later recalled, he "adopted two maxims of conduct," which he recommended to all who should succeed him:

> The first was unreservedly to break with the revolutionary party abroad. . . . But equally I resolved not to let myself be carried on to a denial of the principles of our Revolution: liberty, equality and clemency. I would work for the restoration of order but without ever sharing the passionate feelings of former rulers whom it was in any case impossible to win over; thus France

should, though fighting the revolution, not lose her proper and natural reputation among the nations as a liberal country. . . .

A second maxim was never to attempt anything obviously beyond our powers; never to promise what we could not perform; not to encourage those we could not support, or threaten those we could not strike; in a word, not to aspire to the rank that was ours in other ages but that we could not maintain in the present state of the world, but yet to be proud of the high position that did remain to us, and, facing all risks, to hold that position, should it be disputed.[27]

One can see in these self-admonitions the main outline of Tocqueville's thought: oppose the international revolutionary side of the movement toward democracy but foster liberal institutions within states, have a prudent care for the power France would need to play her part in the balance-of-power game but make it a noble part and be willing to act boldly in its defense.

In the case of the "Roman Question" these general principles were put to a specific test. In the chaos of 1848, an uprising had established a Roman Republic, overthrowing clerical government and forcing the Pope to flee. In the reaction of 1849, with the revolution in retreat everywhere, Pius IX had appealed for outside aid in his restoration, and that summer, only days before Tocqueville accepted the foreign ministry, French troops were despatched to Rome for that purpose. Later, Senior suggested, and Tocqueville agreed, that the motives for the Roman expedition were three: "the maintenance of French influence in Italy, the restoration of the Pope, and the introduction or preservation in Rome of liberal institutions."[28] The expulsion of the Republic was necessary to the defeat of violent revolution in Europe, which would have carried the principle of equality too far. By seeing that the Pope was returned, France gained "a right to be heard" in Italian affairs and forestalled an increased Austrian influence in Italy that would have accompanied that country's intervention. But this was all to be accomplished in a liberal way. The French siege of Rome was carried out so as to avoid undue loss of life and prevent the destruction of the city's architectural and artistic treasures. When this was accomplished, Tocqueville afterwards recalled, "The whole object of my correspondence was to induce the Pope to grant liberal institutions to his people. I considered this as the most important of the three objects of the expedition—as an object affecting not only our interests but our honour, as an object without which the whole expedition was a lamentable failure."[29]   Thus, French diplomats strenuously pressed reluctant papal representatives to reorganize the courts, reform the civil code, establish elective national and municipal councils that would have power over taxation, and replace the ecclesiastical public administration with a secular one. The warrant Tocqueville claimed for demanding reforms was France's reputation before the European society of states; he directed his envoy to remind the pontifical authorities that, "as long as we occupy this territory, we are accountable to the public opinion of Europe and particularly to the public opinion of France, accountable for what takes place within the limits where our army is, and . . . regard for our interest and our honor obliges us strictly not to allow what would wound either."[30]   Louis Napoleon, then president, dismissed the government in which Tocqueville served before the conclusion of these negotiations, but had he remained in office and found himself unable to secure his reformist objectives, he later insisted, he would have withdrawn French forces from the support of the reestablished papal government and published an account of the entire affair as an appeal to posterity. In this way, he said, "We should have set ourselves right with Europe."[31]

Thus, Tocqueville, while he always remained a patriot of his nation, remained as well cognizant of standards of conduct beyond the national.[32]   These two guides to action would produce an international pattern of both assertiveness and moderation—a set of mores that would put bounds on the spread of an undue transnational uniformity, but would foster national progressiveness and self-restraint, in accordance with an enlightened international consensus. If they could be safeguarded against both revolution and reaction, these mores would be vital in preserving national liberty, and through it, individual liberty and civic virtue.

The American Case

For Tocqueville, then, the moral issue in statecraft was two-sided: first, to preserve the state as a focus of loyalty and self-sacrifice that would in turn preserve public spirit among the citizens, and second, to encourage the state to act toward other states and toward the whole society of states in ways that furthered an international consensus on just and honorable state behavior. The correct path through this thicket was not an easy one to find, and the different parts of his analysis could at time point in opposite directions. To judge how the guideposts might direct the United States, we can look to the three factors that he found most helpful in explaining the American regime—mores, circumstances, and laws.

Of the three, Tocqueville found mores to be the most important in preserving a free democratic republic in the United States. America, he thought, was in no immediate danger of seeing public spirit wither in its people; it was perhaps in less danger than any European country even though the principles of equality had progressed further in the New World than anywhere in the Old. "There is a patriotism which mainly springs from the disinterested, undefinable, and unpondered feeling that ties a man's heart to the place where he was born," as Tocqueville described it in *Democracy in America*. "When people are still simple in their mores and firm in their belief, when society gently rests on an ancient order of things whose legitimacy is not contested, then that instinctive patriotism prevails."[33]   Most European countries continued to rely on this sort of patriotism, unaware that its foundation in customs and habits was rapidly disappearing, endangering public spirit and the bulwarks of personal freedom. The American Republic, by contrast, had imbibed from the beginning a newer, "well-considered" patriotism:

> There is another sort of patriotism more rational than [instinctive]; less generous, perhaps less ardent, but more creative and more lasting, it is engendered by enlightenment, grows by the aid of laws and the exercise of rights, and in the end becomes, in a sense, mingled with personal interest. A man understands the influence which his country's well-being has on his own; he knows the law allows him to contribute to the production of this well-being, and he takes an interest in his country's prosperity, first as a thing useful to him and then as something he has created.[34]

This public-spirited turn of mind was further strengthened by the institution of federalism and the decentralization of most governmental authority. For Tocqueville, it was "incontestable that in the United States the taste for and practice in republican government were born in the townships and provincial assemblies," and "that same republican spirit, those same mores and habits of liberty, . . . having come to birth and grown in the various states, are then applied without any trouble in the nation as a whole." Decentralization made the practical benefits of well-considered patriotism more obvious: "In defending the Union, [the citizen] is defending the increasing prosperity of his district, the right to direct its affairs, and the hope of pressing through plans for improvement there which should enrich himself—all things which, in the normal run, touch men more than the general interests of the country and national glory."[35]

Self-interest, combined with federalism, had created a sense of patriotism that, at least for the taste of one visitor, was not only strong but overstrong:

> The American, taking part in everything that is done in his country, feels a duty to defend anything criticized there, for it is not only his country that is being attacked, but himself; hence one finds that his national pride has recourse to every artifice and descends to every childishness of personal vanity.
>
> Nothing is more annoying in the ordinary intercourse of life than this irritable patriotism of the Americans. A foreigner will gladly agree to praise much in their country, but he would like to be allowed to criticize something, and that he is absolutely refused.[36]

The loss of civic virtue in a recognizable national community and its replacement by a combination of a vaguely beneficent attitude toward the whole of humanity and an intensive preoccupation with individual self-interest—this fear was in no appreciable way being realized in the United States. The Americans' national pride was so great that they were more prone to succumb to what Tocqueville thought was a common trait of their English cousins, collective self-righteousness.[37] Moreover, this public spirit was the consequence of domestic conditions, so that there was no need for statesmen to stir up patriotism by embarking on heroic foreign ventures.

Fortunate in its mores, the United States was doubly fortunate in its circumstances. "The American Union has no enemies to fight," Tocqueville observed. "It is as solitary amid the wildernesses as an island in the ocean." A protected geographic setting meant that circumstances did not mandate, any more than mores, an active, glorious role for the United States in its own defense. The lack of formidable nearby enemies released it from the necessities of military rivalry:

> The Americans have no neighbors and conse-
> quently no great wars, financial crises, invasions, or
> conquests to fear; they need neither heavy taxes
> nor a numerous army nor great generals; they have
> also hardly anything to fear from something else
> which is a greater scourge for democratic republics
> than all these others put together, namely, military
> glory.

States confronted by powerful adversaries nearby had to live
with the possibility that a long war for their existence, not
necessarily of their own making, would force them to face a
"sad choice: either defeat will lead them to destruction or
victory will bring them to despotism." The American Union
could be confident it would not "dissolve in the midst of a
great war," because "it has no great wars to fear."[38]
    Secure in its continental isolation, the United States was
a participant in the society of states of the early and mid-19th
century only in a certain sense. Economically and culturally,
it was certainly a part of an "Atlantic Community" by this
time; Tocqueville's own journey and his volumes were
evidence of that.[39] Politically, however, it remained aloof,
outside what he termed in 1853 "the great theatre of human
affairs; for," as he put it, "after all this theatre is not at Sidney,
nor even Washington, it is still in Old Europe."[40]At the same
time, because the United States was a sovereign state granted
diplomatic recognition by the Europeans and because it had
some means of defending itself, it, unlike Asia, could not be
brought into the political system against its will as a colony or
protectorate. Under these circumstances, Tocqueville could
discern no moral obligation for the American Republic to
become an active participant in the society of states, either to
uphold a balance of power or to press the international
consensus on proper state behavior in a progressive direction.
If the United States could maintain civic virtue within its
borders through domestic means, and as long as necessity or
its history did not tie it to the diplomatic combinations of the

Old World, it was free to act or to refrain from acting as it chose. Because of its history and its location, France was intimately bound up with the society of states, for good or ill; Tocqueville once reflected "sadly on the fatal influence which we often exercise upon all around us. When a revolution breaks out in France, all Europe falls into anarchy; and when order is reestablished in France, every other country restores the old abuses."[41] But, in its foreign as in its domestic affairs, the United States began with a clean slate:

> As the Union does not meddle in the affairs of Europe, it has, so to say, no external interests at stake, for as yet it has no powerful neighbors in America. Detached by geography as well as by choice from the passions of the Old World, it neither needs to protect itself against them nor to espouse them. As for those of the New World, they are still hidden in the future.
>
> The Union is free from preexisting obligations; it can therefore profit from the experience of Europe without being obliged, as European nations are, to take the past into account and adapt it to the present; nor need it, like them, accept a vast heritage of mixed glory and shame, national friendship and national hatreds, bequeathed by its ancestors. Expectancy is the keynote of American foreign policy; it consists much more in abstaining than in doing.[42]

"Nations," held Tocqueville, "like individuals who have any self-respect, pledge themselves as to their future conduct by their past."[43] But when nations had no past, he did not consider them irresponsible if they used their freedom of action to stand aside from international society. Rather, he envied them: "How wonderful is the position of the New World, where man has yet no enemies but himself. To be happy and to be free, it is enough to will it to be so."[44]

Still, such fortunate circumstances might not last forever. The growth of the United States' power might lead it to acquire important interests in locations more exposed than its sheltered homeland; powerful empires might arise on its northern or southern borders. It would then quickly discover that its laws were not well suited to a great role in the states-system, for "the great good fortune of the United States is not to have found a federal Constitution enabling them to conduct great wars, but to be so situated that there is nothing for them to fear." If it had a foreign cause for fear, the country would have to reconsider its views on federalism and decentralization:

> No one can appreciate the advantages of a federal system more than I. I hold it to be one of the most powerful combinations favoring human prosperity and freedom. I envy the lot of the nations that have been allowed to adopt it. But yet I refuse to believe that, with equal force on either side, a confederated nation can long fight against a nation with centralized government power.
>
> A nation that divided its sovereignty when faced by the great military monarchies of Europe would seem to me, by that single act, to be abdicating its power, and perhaps its existence and its name.

The distraction of presidential election campaigns and transitions would become less an annoyance, more a hazard: "The more precarious and perilous a nation's position, and the more the need for continuity and stability in the conduct of foreign policy is felt, the more dangerous does the practice of electing the head of state become. . . . There are very few nations in Europe that would not have reason to fear conquest or anarchy every time they provided themselves with a new [elective] leader." While the president and the Senate, the two institutions primarily charged with conducting foreign policy, were less purely democratic than the House of Representatives or the state governments, they were not so far removed from the people as to escape entirely the weaknesses characteristic of any effort to carry out external relations under the influence of public opinion: "a democracy finds it difficult to coordinate the details of a great undertaking and to fix on some plan and carry it through with determination in spite of obstacles. It has little capacity for combining measures in secret and waiting patiently for the result. . . . [It displays a] tendency . . . to obey its feelings rather than its calculations and to abandon a long-matured plan to satisfy a momentary passion."[45]

If it left its isolation, the United States would have a responsibility—perhaps a moral responsibility—to alter its domestic political arrangements so as to be able to play a respectable and constructive part in the greater society of states. It would then encounter with renewed urgency the dilemmas that Tocqueville explored: How to combine individual liberty and civic virtue with national effectiveness on the international stage? How to combine national liberty and vigor with duties to a broader, though intangible, international order? These contrasting imperatives, which Tocqueville may never have fully resolved in his own mind, were worthy of his attention then. They are perennial problems that merit our attention now.

ENDNOTES

1. For selections from and analyses of the writings of these and other observers in the period between the Congress of Vienna and the Crimean War, see M. G. Forsyth, H. M. A. Keens-Soper, and P. Savigear, eds., *The Theory of International Relations: Selected Texts from Gentili to Treitschke* (New York: Atherton Press, 1970), pp. 259-323; Arnold Wolfers and Laurence W. Martin, eds., *The Anglo-American Tradition in Foreign Affairs: Readings from Thomas More to Woodrow Wilson* (New Haven: Yale University Press, 1956), pp. 180-220; F. H. Hinsley, *Power and the Pursuit of Peace: Theory and Practice in the History of Relations between States* (London: Cambridge University Press, 1963), pp. 81-113.

2. The quotations in this and the following two paragraphs are taken from Tocqueville's introduction to volume one of *Democracy in America*, trans. George Lawrence (Garden City, New York: Doubleday, 1969), pp. 9-20.

3. *Journey to America*, ed. J. P. Mayer (New Haven: Yale University Press, 1960), p. 163. See the discussion of this facet of Tocqueville's thought in Marvin Zetterbaum, *Tocqueville and the Problem of Democracy* (Stanford: Stanford University Press, 1967), pp. 149-157.

4. Quoted in Zetterbaum, p. 151.

5. This is the argument suggested by Charles R. Beitz in *Political Theory and International Relations* (Princeton: Princeton University Press, 1979).

6. Quoted in Zetterbaum, p. 150.

7. *Democracy in America*, 1: 224.

8. Letter to Madame Swetchine, 20 October 1856, in *Memoir, Letters, and Remains of Alexis de Tocqueville*, 2 vols. (London: Macmillan and Company, 1861), 2: 349-350. See also Zetterbaum, p. 151.

9. Letter of 18 December 1840, in *Memoir*, 2: 62-63.

10. See Roger Boesche, *The Strange Liberalism of Alexis de Tocqueville* (Ithaca, New York: Cornell University Press, 1987), pp. 215-218.

11. Letter to the Baron and Baroness de Tocqueville, 6 April 1830, in *Memoir*, 1: 443.

12. Letter to Lady Teresa Lewis, 18 October 1857, in *Memoir*, 2: 409.

13. Letter to Henry Reeve, 12 April 1840, ibid., pp. 53-54.

14. *Democracy in America*, 2: 649.

15. See Boesche, pp. 218-225.

16. *Democracy in America*, 1: 12.

17. Letter of 9 March 1952, in *Memoir*, 2: 201-202.

18. Letter of 15 February 1855, Ibid., p. 293.

19. Quoted in Mary Lawlor, "Alexis de Tocqueville in the Chamber of Deputies: His Views on Foreign and Colonial Policy" (Ph.D. dissertation, The Catholic University of America, 1959), p. 82.

20. *Memoir*, 2: 215.

21. Letter of 16 September 1855, in *Memoir*, 2: 310.

22. *Democracy in America*, 1: 161.

23. *Memoir*, 2: 8; Tocqueville: *Souvenirs*, quoted in Edward T. Gargan, *Alexis de Tocqueville: The Critical Years 1848-1851* (Washington, D.C.: The Catholic University of America Press, 1955), pp. 145-146.

24. Letter to Reeve, 22 May 1836, in *Memoir*, 2: 24. Of course, Tocqueville was not always uncritical of Great Britain. See Lawlor, pp. 67-99; Boesche, p. 216.

25. Letter to M. de Corcelle, 11 October 1846, in *Memoir*, 2: 79.

26. See Lawlor, pp. 150-170.

27. Alexis de Tocqueville, *Recollections*, trans. George Lawrence, eds. J. P. Mayer and R. P. Kerr (Garden City, New York: Doubleday, 1970), pp. 240-241.

28. Extracts from the journal of Nassau Senior, 17 February 1851, in *Memoir*, 2: 148.

29. Ibid., 2: 151.

30. Quoted in Gargan, p. 161.

31. *Memoir*, 2: 155. The entire Roman episode is discussed in *Memoir*, 2: 148-155 and Gargan, pp. 122-179. Tocqueville's speech on the Roman expedition, given before the National Assembly on 18 October 1849, less than two weeks before he was to leave office, is reprinted in *Recollections*, pp. 296-313.

32. See the letter to Baron Tocqueville, 7 March 1854 in *Memoir*, 2: 263.

33. 1: 235.

34. Ibid., pp. 235-236.

35. Ibid., 1: 162.

36. Ibid., 1: 237. See also 2: 612-614.

37. See the letter to Harriet Grote, 31 January 1857, in *Memoir*, 2: 365-367.

38. *Democracy in America*, 1: 306, 278, 168, 169. See also Appendix O, pp. 726-727.

39. For a discussion of transatlantic ties in this period, see Paul A. Varg, *United States Foreign Relations, 1820-1860* (East Lansing, Michigan: Michigan State University Press, 1979), pp. 20-42.

40. Letter to Henry Reeve, March 1853, in *Memoir*, 2: 216.

41. Letter to M. Dufaure, 22 December 1850, ibid., 2: 124.

42. *Democracy in America*, 1: 228.

43. Letter to Reeve, March 1853, in *Memoir*, 2: 216-217.

44. *Democracy in America*, 1: 170.

45. Ibid., 1: 170, 131, 229.

II.

PROBLEMS OF CONTEMPORARY PRESIDENTIAL RHETORIC

CHAPTER 2

FDR's Presidential Rhetoric

HALFORD RYAN

NARRATOR: We've had a series of discussions at the Miller Center on the history and development of rhetoric. They began with an examination of rhetoric in Greek times, Roman times, and medieval times. Then we addressed specific problems, such as the rhetoric of public diplomacy. Altogether, there are 20 volumes in this series, and we reach the culmination and purpose of these discussions with the topic of presidential rhetoric. We are trying to draw on what we learned about the foundations of rhetoric to analyze modern presidential rhetoric.

I was never so aware of how vital this had become as when listening to the discussions of some members of a Harvard commission on presidential press conferences. In that discussion Richard Darman and others who served in the White House during Reagan's first term talked about the infinite care and attention that President Reagan gave to preparations for speeches, press conferences, and other appearances. They said that the briefings which concerned him most were the preparations for his presentations rather than the substance. He insisted that he rehearse these presentations over and over again so that, as he put it, "I get it right." Rhetoric, style, and format have come to the fore in presidential communication, perhaps because of the media.

Halford Ryan is professor of speech at Washington and Lee University. In a sense he is returning to the University of Virginia because he was previously a visiting professor of speech at U.Va. He was born in Anderson, Indiana, and received his bachelor's degree at Wabash College and his master's and Ph.D. at the University of Illinois. He has taught at Sweet Briar and at Virginia Military Institute. He is the author of *Franklin D. Roosevelt's Rhetorical Presidency*; *American Rhetoric from Roosevelt to Reagan: A Collection of Speeches and Critical Essays*; with Bernard Duffy, a book called *American Orators of the Twentieth Century: Critical Studies and Sources*, and *American Orators Before 1900*; and his own *Oratorical Encounters: Selected Studies and Sources of Twentieth Century Political Accusations and Apologies* with fascinating essays entitled, "Nixon's Apology for the Fund" and "Prime Minister Stanley Baldwin Versus King Edward VIII." He has also written *Harry Emerson Fosdick: Persuasive Preacher*, and *Henry Ward Beecher: Stump Preacher*.

PROFESSOR RYAN: The purpose of my recent book was to examine FDR's rhetorical presidency, and I had some hidden purposes in it. What I wanted to do in my book, in a roundabout way, was to suggest that rhetorical technique, that is, persuasive ability, or the art of rhetoric, can, as a matter of fact, gain and maintain presidential power. My work is, as a matter of fact, a study of rhetorical technique. For example, Ronald Reagan's method is a very good example of rhetorical technique that worked rather well.

James Ceaser co-authored an important article in *Presidential Studies Quarterly*, entitled "The Rhetorical Presidency." The basic thesis is that the president delivers rhetoric for two reasons: (1) to persuade the people to elect him; and (2) to move the people to move the Congress to enact his agenda. He does that, of course, through programmatic speeches addressed to the American people and to the Congress. These are basically the two departure points for my book.

Specifically, I wanted to show that FDR practiced the art of rhetoric for success. He used speech purposefully; he wanted to persuade people. And so looking at his rhetoric, we see how successful he was. Secondly, I tried to explain the idea of "rhetorical revisionism." The important question is what makes a speech successful. A critic should indicate what elements of presentation make a speech successful or unsuccessful. Then one needs to go the next step and suggest that the speech should have been done according to the art. The critic must say that it should have been done this way, or that it could have been more successful if it were done that way. I apply this rhetorical revisionism particularly when I address the court fight and the purge.

I purposefully began the book with a chapter on persuasive delivery. Generally, if the topic of delivery is treated at all, it is at the back of a book. I wanted to put a chapter on persuasion at the beginning of the book. FDR's delivery was extremely persuasive and compelling.

This past summer I received a grant from the Hoover Library Association to research Herbert Hoover's speech delivery. I went to Long Branch and viewed all of Hoover's extant speeches that are on newsreel. Herbert Hoover would deliver a 75- or 80-page speech text, which literally would go up on a music stand. It was at eye level because he wanted to deliver his speeches like that. So they put the speech text up there, and he would literally look out at the audience. And one by one he would read the pages aloud. He would literally read the speech from the text with no inflections. I never saw the man gesture once. He just stood there, statue-like, and delivered his speeches, with little inflection and no dynamism, in his own dour manner. The evidence suggests that his delivery was not compelling.

Juxtapose his style to that of FDR with the smile, the raised hand, the grin, the inflection, and the dynamism. It was a comparison that anyone could see without any difficulty.

FDR paid a lot of attention to the delivery of his speeches. For instance, he would mark how long they were going to last; he would underline phrases for emphasis and what would be accentuated when he actually delivered the speech. In short, he paid attention to the delivery of his speeches in the speech invention process.

The other thing that I did was to sit down in the FDR Library and go through the White House files on the public reaction to FDR's speeches. This work is boring and tedious, and the dust gets in your eyes, but occasionally you find some useful letters. Most of the letters say "good luck" and "wonderful job," and that kind of thing. Now and then, though, one can get some substantive comments from Americans who reacted specifically to Roosevelt's rhetorical technique and his delivery. I utilized these sources whenever I could. You have to spend about 30 minutes to get one useful letter, but once you have that, it provides real insight. Americans did react positively to his delivery.

The next topic I discussed was FDR and the media. Roosevelt was not the first to utilize the radio, but here again the radio was very effective for reaching the mass audience, and he had a wonderful radio voice. By comparison, Hoover didn't.

I treated the press conferences, as one would expect, and I did try to study the newsreels. I argued that presidential rhetorical critics ought to utilize the newsreels. There is not much substance on the newsreels, but Americans sitting in a movie theater saw him there even if they missed his speeches. New Dealers, when they learned that an FDR newsreel was going to be at the movies, would go down to the movie house to cheer FDR, and Republicans would go down to hiss him.

The newsreels were the 1930s equivalent of television: Americans saw FDR enacting his speeches and enacting his presidency. Some early critics in the 1930s understood very well what the newsreel did. One person said that the content of the speech was less important than what is seen. Note the importance of seeing. I suppose that runs counter to critics who want to pay attention to the substance of the rhetoric. But the fact is that people reacted to those visual cues.

The other rhetorical technique that I found in the media was the "scapegoat" that FDR liked to utilize. He was not the first to use it and neither has he been the last to apply it, but he utilized the news media as a scapegoat. When things weren't going well, particularly in the purge and the court fight, he would abuse the news media. That would divert attention from his problems and would transfer them to his scapegoat, the "Tory press," that nice aristocratic metaphor. People would focus on the Tory press and forget about FDR's problems. Carter, Ford, and Reagan have utilized it too, so it is nothing new.

The next chapter in the book covers four campaigns. He isolated four basic stances that both rival candidates and incumbent presidents take: *attack, defense, ignore*, and "*me too, me better.*" These served very well in the analysis of the four campaigns, and although FDR did not debate, I discovered some interesting rhetorical strategies.

I looked broadly at FDR's 1932 campaign. In his first campaign, of course, Roosevelt's basic stance was attack. Incumbents generally are cast into the role of defense while the candidates who are not in office usually are the attacker. One gets from FDR a very good idea of problems in the Hoover administration, but one does not get a very clear idea about Roosevelt's ideas or where he thought the country ought to go. Basically, Roosevelt ran a campaign by negation. He was not for this or that; he was not for Hooverism. It was not very clear what he was *for*, though, which was an opportunity that was afforded him by being out of office rather than the incumbent. Hoover was cast in the role of defending his administration, which is exactly what Roosevelt wanted him to do. It also gave Roosevelt some latitude. If he was not very specific, then he could not be counterattacked by his opposition, so he just waffled on lots of issues.

Roosevelt ran a good campaign by employing persuasive metaphors. You know the "forgotten man" speech, a metaphor that everyone could identify with, because almost everyone thought he was the forgotten man under the Hoover administration. The Hoover administration replied with its famous metaphor attacking Roosevelt. Hoover described Roosevelt's policies on balancing the budget and tariffs as being akin to a "chameleon on plaid." Think about that. How can a chameleon react on plaid? Hoover's was a very intellectual metaphor, but it was not a visceral metaphor like the forgotten man. One can easily identify with a forgotten man, but not a chameleon. Hoover utilized metaphors, but they did not sell as Roosevelt's did.

Next came FDR's New Deal speech and the Commonwealth Club address, which was a nod to the business community. Then there was the Pittsburgh speech where he said he was "going to balance the budget"; in 1936 he came to regret that he ever gave that speech. Sam Rosenman reread that speech and said, "Mr. President, you just might as well forget that you gave that speech; you can't defend yourself on that one at all."

We know now, of course, that Hoover lost. Roosevelt certainly did not act as if he knew that would happen. He campaigned very vigorously. Hoover did not act as if the campaign were foregone because he emerged from what we would call today a "Rose Garden" strategy and delivered a number of campaign speeches across the country.

The point that we miss in hindsight is that both of these men did participate in and thereby define the rhetorical presidency. They took their campaigns directly to the people. Hoover originally was not going to do that, and then his advisers said, as one Supreme Court justice told him, "Mr. President, remember that the American people do elect the president." That fact was unfortunate for Hoover.

Roosevelt's 1936 campaign was the beginning of a new campaign strategy for him, which he basically used in his third and fourth campaigns as well. I called it an aggressive defense. What Roosevelt did was to run against Hooverism;

he never mentioned Landon by name. It was more effective to run against Hoover in 1936 than Landon.

Roosevelt pursued the strategy of waiting for the Republicans to attack. The Republicans basically ran a two-pronged campaign: they ran an "attack" campaign and a "me too, me better" campaign. First, they claimed that they could do everything that the New Deal was doing, but that they would do it better. The assertion that Republicans would do it better than Democrats was really not very persuasive. And "the attack", of course, was not very useful either because the New Deal seemed at that time to be overcoming the Depression. So what Roosevelt did was to wait until he was attacked by the Landon campaign and then respond vigorously to the attack, which was a very astute strategy. Rather than going out and campaigning *for* things, which is like saying to Landon, "Here, attack me on this," he waited and responded to specific attacks for which he had persuasive responses. He did not have to defend those things that he did not broach, so he rarely sounded defensive. It was a beautiful campaign strategy.

I would like to read to you from his Syracuse speech. It suggests how he turned the tables on the Republicans. He said:

> Let me warn you, let me warn the nation against the smooth evasion which says, 'Of course we believe in all of these things. We believe in social security; we believe in work for the unemployed; we believe in saving homes. Cross our hearts and hope to die. We believe in all these things. We do not like the way the present administration is doing them; just turn them over to us. We will do all of them; we will do more of them; we will do them better; and most of all, the doing of them will not cost anybody anything.'

The audience just howled with delight, and Roosevelt campaigned all over the country with that appeal. It was not chicanery and it was not show business; it was the truth. The Republicans' "me, too, me better" strategy was not going to work, and the attack didn't work either. So the 1936 campaign was his most interesting and probably his best campaign. He had his biggest landslide in 1936.

In the third campaign, Roosevelt tried to utilize the same strategy against Wendell Willkie. However, Willkie had one up on Landon; Willkie had a pretty good radio voice, and Willkie tried the basic strategy of attacking the New Deal. He tried to attack the idea of a third term, but that was not a contentious issue. So Willkie finally went for "the troops are almost already on the transports to Europe" approach. Roosevelt countered in the best way that a president could: he just got on the train and went to look at all the munitions factories up and down the East Coast. These visits were on the newsreel, so here was the President looking at all the airplanes, tanks, and ships. Here, again, Roosevelt basically adopted an aggressive defense. He waited for Willkie to attack and then either responded verbally or with these presidential images. The race was a little bit closer that time around.

In the fourth campaign Dewey was probably every bit as good in terms of his radio delivery and in his radio presence as FDR. Many critics suggested that this was the first time that FDR competed with a "media person" who could meet FDR on his own ground. He probably realized that and decided to campaign vigorously.

The speech that immediately comes to mind is the Teamster's Union address. There was a rhetorical efficacy in the Teamster's Union address that people have not realized. Roosevelt needed to invigorate the campaign with some kind of excitement, partly because the war was going on and people were getting tired of it. What better way to do that than to interject humor into the campaign? Only Franklin Delano Roosevelt could utilize humor on such a serious topic in a

serious campaign and bring it off. And, of course, here was
Roosevelt's rhetorical acumen. Who was the humorless man?
Who was the plastic groom on the wedding cake? Dewey was
the dour man, and Roosevelt attacked that quality in the
speech. This speech invigorated a war-weary world with some
good, old-fashioned campaign rhetoric.

Of more substance was the issue of the United Nations.
Left over from the 1940 campaign were the Willkie internationalists, who were sort of a swing vote. Would they go
with Roosevelt or with Dewey? Dewey missed an opportunity
on the United Nations issue, the question Senator Joseph H.
Ball and the internationalists were concerned about. Would
the U.S. commit forces to the United Nations under
international control for a peacekeeping mission or would
Congress decide? What is the United States' position on
that?

Dewey, not wanting to alienate the isolationists in his
own party, glossed over the issue. Roosevelt, in reminiscence
of the "garden hose analogy" that he used to support lend-
lease, suggested—he did not *say* he would do this, but he used
the metaphor to imply it—that the police constable does not
go down to the town hall to swear out a warrant for an arrest
when he sees a criminal entering a house to commit a crime.
The metaphor did not say what he was going to do. It
suggested though that he would be in support of committing
American forces, and that metaphor was enough for Ball and
his camp to swing to Roosevelt. Roosevelt's command of
metaphor at a critical moment was useful for his campaign.

I next examined the four inaugural addresses. I utilized
an important essay published in *Presidential Studies Quarterly*,
titled "Inaugurating the Presidency," by Kathleen Jamieson
from the University of Texas (who is often quoted in
Newsweek about presidential rhetoric) and Karlyn Kohrs
Campbell from the University of Minnesota. They claimed
that there are four elements in presidential inaugural
addresses. The first is that the president "reconstitutes" the
people. After a divisive campaign, the president brings the

people together in the inaugural address. Secondly, he rehearses American communal values: God, mother, apple pie–the kind of stock appeals that one finds in every presidential inaugural address. Thirdly, the president communicates the broad political principles that will inform his administration. The president will not specify every piece of legislation that he is going to propose in the next four years. He will communicate those political principles that will guide him. And then fourthly, he needs to stress his powers and limitations. He cannot be perceived as a wimp, having no powers whatsoever, as Carter was perceived by some in his inaugural. On the other hand the president cannot say, "I shall enact the imperial presidency." So he has to walk a tightrope in stressing his powers but also acknowledging his limitations. Finally, all of this is accomplished in epideictic rhetoric, which is a technical term in speech that denotes ceremonial speeches that are given on state occasions. In my book, with regard to FDR's four inaugurals, I took the Jamieson and Campbell essay to task.

My initial interest in FDR's inaugural addresses was his first inaugural. I found that he utilized three rhetorical techniques that make this an extremely persuasive speech, and probably one of the best speeches he ever delivered. It certainly was the first or second best inaugural address that was ever delivered.

He–actually he, Raymond Moley, and Louis Howe, the other people who helped him write the speech–isolated three important audiences. The first device that he utilized was the military metaphor. He had to stir up the people to believe the Depression was a war-like situation. The speech is filled with military metaphors. Why did he use them? He needed to enlist the American people in a metaphorical battle against the Depression. Why did he use a battle image? Well, in the military, one gives up some freedoms for the common good. That's exactly what Roosevelt wanted the American people to do. No more laissez-faire government–the government would intervene in our lives. He told the people that they should join the "army" to fight the Depression, and it followed that they would therefore have to give up some of the freedoms they enjoyed before the Depression.

Second, he utilized the "scapegoat" technique. In his New Deal speech he said that Americans played the stock market and were partly responsible for the Depression. Now a president should never tell the American electorate that they are at fault. Jimmy Carter tried that on the energy crisis and he fell flat. However, Roosevelt used the "scapegoat" technique on the Wall Streeters, particularly the bankers. They caused the Depression. The electorate responded positively. Roosevelt drove the money changers from the temple and asserted that with the scapegoat driven out, the American people could reenter the temple with their sins cleansed. Also note that the Wall Streeters were to be regulated, or at least FDR told the people he would regulate them.

The last device that he utilized was "the carrot and the stick" strategy. When he fashioned his inaugural address, he did not know he was going to be as successful as he was, so he utilized the carrot and the stick. He communicated to the Congress that he wanted to work with them. If the Congress were not forthcoming, then he would go to the people and ask for broad power to meet the crisis. The irony of the strategy was that if Congress would not cooperate with him in the first instance, they were certainly not going to cooperate in giving him broad executive power. But Americans did not think about that. Rather, the image FDR conveyed was that if the Congress did not cooperate, he would go over its head to the people. That motivated the Congress, rhetorically at least, to cooperate with the president. This was the classic tenet of taking the presidency directly to the people to move the Congress.

To move to the Supreme Court fight, I may encounter some questioning of my views. I developed a theory of accusation and apology in which I suggested that speeches of accusation motivate speeches of apology. I looked at the court fight from this rhetorical standpoint. There are many caveats that I do not have time to list, and I realize that other factors were present. But here is where my rhetorical revisionism comes in. I argued that Roosevelt advanced a bogus argument against the Supreme Court in his judiciary message, namely that it was overburdened, overworked, and overaged. That was not a very good accusation, and the Republicans just sat back and let some conservative Democrats attack FDR, which they did. It was true that the justices were old, but that didn't necessarily imply that they were overworked or that they were conservative. So the old-age, overburdened argument backfired.

Sensing his mistake, Roosevelt delivered two of his better speeches: the "Victory Dinner" address and the fireside chat on the judiciary. In the Victory Dinner address, he dropped the old-age, overburdened argument and argued instead that the real problem was a conservative Supreme Court that was thwarting the ability of the Congress and the executive to meet problems of a national depression with national legislation. (That is what he ought to have said in the beginning.) In the fireside chat on the judiciary, FDR lapsed back into the old-age, overburdened argument. The people were not persuaded.

I do not claim that FDR would have won the Supreme Court fight if he had adopted my revisionism. I do believe that he would have been more successful from a rhetorical point of view had he preempted some of the accusations that he received. For support of my argument, I used as an analogue Chief Justice Charles Evans Hughes' letter to the Senate Judiciary Committee. There is a compelling interrelationship between that letter and FDR's speech.

Hughes met Roosevelt head on and said, "The Court is not now overburdened or overworked," and used statistical evidence to suggest that the Court had heard and disposed of more cases under Roosevelt than it had under the Hoover administration. It was patently false that the Court was overworked and overburdened. Hughes, on two occasions, specifically said, "I do not address propositions of policy on what position the Court ought to take vis-à-vis the legislation." There is the proof for what I contend. Hughes would have been cast into a role of defending the court's conservative interpretation, which he did not want to do. If Roosevelt had straightforwardly attacked the conservative court, Hughes would have been constrained in his responses. He would have had either to remain silent or try to defend the conservatism. We know in hindsight that Hughes did not want to bother defending conservatism because the court had changed in late December, but he didn't communicate that to Roosevelt, and Roosevelt didn't know it.

So my rhetorical revisionism suggests that Roosevelt should have made a frontal attack. Roosevelt should have broached the Court problem in his second inaugural in terms of political principles. This approach would have avoided much of the surprise he sprung on the country.

Let me move to the purge. In a chapter entitled "The War of Words and Words of War," I argue for rhetorical revisionism of the purge. It is also a classic example of where the rhetorical presidency does not work. There were some real problems in the purge from a conceptual point of view. The American people accepted the president's programmatic speeches for national issues, but Roosevelt didn't appreciate the unwritten separation of powers doctrine.

I utilized the theory of accusation regarding a speech against Roosevelt given by Senator Walter George. FDR's only comment about Senator George was that "deep down in his heart he's not a New Deal liberal." What did that attack allow George to do in his response? George countered with black-baiting, opposition to labor unions, and other extraneous issues, but this was very effective with the Georgia audience. Senator George said that Roosevelt never spelled out a "bill of particulars."

Roosevelt should have attacked George, Representative John J. O'Connor, Senator Millard Tydings, and others on the basis of a single litmus test—the New Deal. FDR should have attacked their stance on the New Deal, not whether in their hearts they were liberal or conservative. Of course, the purge did not work, and it might not have worked as I suggested it might have, but he certainly could have handled it much better than he did.

NARRATOR: Could I begin by asking about Lou Cannon's column yesterday [5 September 1988]? He criticized Vice President Bush for doing what Cannon said President Reagan never did, namely, to impugn the patriotism of his opponent. Cannon said that you put yourself on a tightrope if you challenge the patriotism of your opponent. Is that borne out in terms of peacetime situations? Do wartime situations change that dramatically?

PROFESSOR RYAN: I'm not going to answer your question directly, but I'll give you an example to illustrate Roosevelt's technique. In the wartime situation Roosevelt used an incredible line in the 1940 campaign. He said something like this: "Now, I'm not accusing the noninterventionists and the isolationists of aiding and abetting the Nazi administration, but what they are doing is aiding and abetting the Nazi administration." Roosevelt did not directly attack the patriotism of people. He had a more artful way of doing it.

NARRATOR: Norman Graebner, you taught a course on Roosevelt when you were Harmsworth Professor of American History at Oxford. Are there issues that came up in your discussions there that we ought to consider here?

PROFESSOR GRAEBNER: I certainly did dwell on the rhetoric of Roosevelt because it was so effective, and you can't deal with Roosevelt without paying attention to his voice and gestures and so on. But there is the other side to this that I would like to raise, namely, the nature of the audience which you are addressing. You spoke largely of the person doing the speaking and his techniques, which were all extremely effective. I've listened to many of those speeches myself, and I have to admit that they were unbelievably effective. But he was addressing audiences that were going to react very positively to his rhetoric. There was a connection between what he was saying about economic royalists, for example, and the fact that several million people were unemployed, and that several million others were holding on as best they could. There was an audience that was going to react very positively to what he said.

You also talked about Hoover's lack of success and use of rhetoric. Until the Depression hit, Hoover went over very well. In other words, what is changing in the decline of Hoover's rhetoric is not his sudden loss of ability, but the fact that his audience had changed. After 1929 he was getting stones thrown at him for the same speech that would have brought nothing but applause two years earlier. So I am wondering if you would comment on the relationship between the audience and the reaction. Reagan gets extremely positive results in his speeches but usually before handpicked audiences. Having taught for 40 years, I know that you cannot stand before an audience successfully unless the audience is on your side.

PROFESSOR RYAN: You've raised a valid question. The fireside chats have always been conceived as single-issue speeches: Roosevelt "going before the nation" in the fireside chats. I tried to argue specifically in the book that they were not devoted to one topic. In both the chats and in all of his other speeches, Roosevelt addressed a multiplicity of audiences. The fireside chat on the judiciary in 1937 addressed other issues. Roosevelt tried to address as many audiences as he could in those speeches.

Obviously Roosevelt was not going to persuade the 16 million hard-core Republicans who voted for Landon, but there were Republicans who took a walk. I have a number of quotations from Republicans who, after listening to a speech, sided with FDR. He knew that more people were going to read his speeches in the newspapers, and so the style and the rhetorical appeals were utilized for their reading value as well. It is difficult to conceptualize *the* American audience.

PROFESSOR CLAUDE: I am wondering whether presidential rhetoric has become increasingly important as the 20th century has gone on because of the development of the electronic and photographic media as compared with the 19th century when not many people could see a president or hear him in person. By contrast congressional rhetoric has become less important. You hear less about Daniel Websters in the Senate these days than in the 19th century. Is it true that we've had this contrasting pair of trends?

PROFESSOR RYAN: Clearly the answer is yes but only to a certain degree. Nineteenth-century presidents did not give as many programmatic speeches to the American people. The first so-called "rhetorical president" was either Theodore Roosevelt or Woodrow Wilson.

A questionable claim about the rhetorical presidency that Ceaser and his co-authors made is that presidential communications to the people move the Congress. I do not want to say that Reagan is not a successful presidential persuader, but if you look at it, did he really persuade the Congress to pass Reaganomics or did he simply have a very favorable Congress to begin with? Did he simply use rhetoric that reinforced the opinions of the people who had already elected him? Let's talk about Roosevelt. He was elected by huge majorities, but it is not clear whether his rhetoric caused that. In two instances, the purge and the court fight, he was not persuasive.

QUESTION: I wonder if you might give us some idea of the division of labor that went in putting together a speech of Roosevelt's. Who were the speech writers? Who worked on substance? Who added the clever phrase? How much did FDR himself insert in terms of rhetoric?

PROFESSOR RYAN: The first among equals and the pivotal person was Samuel Rosenman. Rosenman wrote a lot of the speeches. Stanley High, Donald Richberg, Thomas Corcoran, Louis Howe, Adolf Berle, and many others also contributed.

People are very concerned about ghostwriters, the man behind the throne. I argued that such concerns are silly. Roosevelt took a lot of time with his drafts. He went over them, changed the style, practiced and read them. He must have read them aloud or at least to himself because he had the minutes ticked off and knew how long the speeches were. For all intents and purposes, they were Roosevelt's speeches.

The third inaugural address was basically his. It started out in his own handwriting, but he was not particularly eloquent. The third inaugural address was a kind of second-rate speech because it was basically Roosevelt's speech. On the other hand, the phrase "I see one-third of a nation," was Roosevelt's and so was almost all of the Pearl Harbor war message. So from time to time he produced oratorical gems. Rosenman's oral biography suggests that oftentimes speech writers did make policies. Roosevelt said, "I have to have a speech; please write a speech for me." But Roosevelt would read the speech and make emendations, so the addresses were *his*.

NARRATOR: We hope that our connections both with an individual scholar at Washington and Lee and with the institution is one we can carry further. We look forward to his next visit.

CHAPTER 3

A Speech Writer on Humor and the Public

ROBERT ORBEN

NARRATOR: Bob Orben has written that humor is one of the glories of human experience. It warms, amuses, instructs, and opens emotional doors. Maybe that is one of the reasons we are very pleased that he would visit us. He was the director of President Ford's speech writing department. He is the editor of Orben's Current Comedy, a humor service for public speakers published in Wilmington, Delaware. He is a consultant, a speech writer, and adviser to entertainment personalities, political leaders, and business chief executives. He wrote scripts for the "Jack Paar Show" and for the "Red Skelton Hour." He is the author of a number of works including the *Encyclopedia of One Liner Comedy*.

MR. ORBEN: There are 46 books altogether. Even I don't try to remember the titles.

NARRATOR: Anyway, he has done all of this. He is now a member of the group that for months, I have been told, was hush-hush, nobody wanted to admit that it existed, but *Time* magazine evidently unveiled them in a recent issue. This is the group of presidential speech writers who had their first meeting last Friday at Bill Safire's home in Washington. So he is recognized not only by people who are desperate for something to say to women's clubs, but he is highly regarded by his own peers, namely, former speech writers. He was close to President Ford; he was his consultant and special assistant. He is one of the people who surely doesn't need any introduction because from now on it is going to become less heavy, less boring, and less pedantic than most discussions, especially the discussions of the converted speaking to the converted.

MR. ORBEN: One of the things you should be aware of is just as the shoemaker's children are poorly shod, you should never ask a speech writer to come with a prepared speech. They just don't do it. What I've done is put together what speech writers call some "talking points" and they will get me started. Then if at any time during what I'm saying or after you have questions, jump in and we'll tackle them on the spot. Of the 12 or 13 specific questions that I received, I'm truly able to answer only a few of them because speech writers, in spite of their own desire to appear to themselves and the world very important, are merely spear carriers in the operation. Our whole responsibility is to put the president's words or client's words into a form that is appealing and recognizable to audiences. And so, overwhelmingly, we're not advisers, we're not movers and shakers, we're spear carriers. Please keep that in mind in light of whatever I say.

One of the questions I'm often asked is: "How does someone go from being a Hollywood television writer to writing speeches for the president of the United States?" That was always a much more intriguing question until a Hollywood television actor became president of the United States. So it isn't all that unusual any more.

My story goes back to 1964. As Ken indicated, I had written at that time perhaps 25 or 30 books on the uses of humor by public speakers, performers, and political figures, in addition to writing for show business personalities. And so in 1964 I found myself with three major responsibilities: I was a writer on the "Red Skelton Show," one of eight writers—I was the one who did the monologue on the show, the one that always ended with Gertrude and Heathcliff, the two sea gulls, talking to each other; I was also at that point sending a page of material a day to Dick Gregory, the activist comedian; and I was sending a page of material a day to Senator Barry Goldwater, who was then running for President of the United States. People always ask me, are jokes interchangeable? Well, obviously not. Each time I sat down to the typewriter I would have to put on my thinking cap as one of the three personalities and write from that viewpoint.

As you remember from reading the papers, Barry Goldwater did not make it, and I went on for four more years as one of the writers on the "Red Skelton Show." We now fast-forward to 1968, another presidential year. I'll attempt to give you a little background that you may or may not be aware of relative to political personalities in Washington. If you put together a job description for presidents of the United States or a congressman or a senator, you would put down a born leader, a great communicator, a good legislator, and all those good things. But you would also in this day and age have to put down the capacity to be a good stand-up comedian, because there are at least a dozen events in Washington where the President of the United States, if he is a savvy President of the United States, will appear and do eight to ten minutes of stand-up comedy à la Johnny Carson. One of the most prestigious of these events is the Gridiron Dinner held in March or April of each year. It gathers together 600 of the movers and shakers in this country: the top CEOs of large corporations, the leading political figures, the Supreme Court justices, all in all a very prestigious audience. Political fortunes have been made and destroyed by good or inept performances.

At a recent event in Washington, I reminded Clark Clifford, who wrote for Harry Truman, that we once shared seats at a Gridiron Dinner. I had said to Clark Clifford at that dinner, "You know, coming from Hollywood I'm rather astonished how important people here in Washington feel this Gridiron Dinner is." I said, "In Hollywood we have a roast every other day and people really don't attribute that much importance to them." And he said, "Well, the value of the Gridiron Dinner is this: if any of the political figures gave a serious speech, you would pretty much know where they are coming from, what they would be saying. The question is, how would these political figures conduct themselves in a situation that's alien to them? What could be more alien to a rock-solid political figure than standing up and doing eight minutes of comedy? It's a very intimidating bit of business." And so, Washington judges the political figures on how well they react to this emergency situation.

At any rate, back to 1968. The format of the Gridiron Dinner is that in addition to sketches they pick one leading Democrat and one leading Republican, and each is required to do eight to ten minutes of stand-up comedy. In 1968 the leading Democrat chosen was Vice President Hubert Humphrey, who was very adept at the uses of humor. The leading Republican was Congressman and Minority Leader of the House of Representatives Gerald R. Ford. Congressman Ford gave many speeches but he really didn't use humor to any great extent, and so it was felt that it might be profitable to get some professional help. I have to preface this by saying I'm not a note taker nor a diary keeper, so I may be wrong in the actual details of this. But as I understand it, Bob Hartmann, the chief of staff for Congressman Ford, came out to California to ask Senator George Murphy, the former movie star and then senator of California, for help. Senator George Murphy sent him to Red Skelton; Red Skelton sent him to the producer of the show; the producer of the show, Sy Berns, sent him to me as the monologue writer on the show and the only card-carrying Republican on the writing staff, if not in all of Hollywood. So I wound up writing a good part of Congressman Ford's Gridiron Dinner speech. In a way I think Congressman Ford was stuck with me because Bob Hartmann came out to Hollywood with two names: one was Senator George Murphy to look up, and if that didn't work out, the other name was somebody who had been sending a lot of material to Barry Goldwater back in 1964, me. So one way or another they were stuck with me.

It proved to be a turning point speech in many ways for Congressman Ford in that Washingtonians had thought it was going to be a wipeout in this battle of humor. Congressman Ford wasn't given much of a chance to excel over Vice President Humphrey and after it was over, it was generally considered that Ford had scored more points than Humphrey had. The thing that I remember most about the speech was the amazingly prophetic finish of Congressman Ford's Gridiron speech. To set the scene, it was March or April of 1968. The presidential campaign was heating up. Lyndon Johnson had already dropped out of the race, so the nomination on both sides of the aisle was up for grabs. There were probably at least a dozen people in that audience who had their eye on the nomination. As Congressman Ford finished his speech, he looked over the group and acknowledged this situation—and then he turned to Hubert Humphrey, who was obviously the leading Democratic possibility, and solemnly assured the vice president that he, Jerry Ford, had absolutely no designs on the White House. He said, "I love the House of Representatives, despite the long, irregular hours. Sometimes though, when it's late and I'm tired and hungry and taking that long drive back to Alexandria, Virginia, as I go past 1600 Pennsylvania Avenue I do seem to hear a little voice within me saying, 'If you lived here, you'd be home now.'" And just six years later he was.

When he became vice president in 1973, I was taken on as a consultant, and then about eight or nine days after he became President, I was called down to be a speech writer, and eventually wound up as director of the speech writing department.

The next question is, how are presidential speeches written? How were they written in the Ford administration? From the standpoint of personnel, we had six speech writers including myself, four researchers, three secretaries—a department of about 13 people. We had, in retrospect, and in talking to other presidential speech writers, amazing access to the President. I took it for granted at the time since I had never worked face to face with a president before. I had done other high-level political writing but never on staff. I just assumed this was the norm. On average we met twice a week for roughly one hour a meeting. One hour would be devoted to going over the schedule of events coming up in which the President would have to speak. Before I took over, Paul Theis, who was the executive editor and head of the speech writers, would bring in three options for every speech. These represented the speech writers' observations on what might be said in the speech. But it was always the President who made the key decisions. He either went with one of the options or told us, "No, I don't want to do that. This is the area we should cover." So we left this one-hour session, knowing where we were going on every major speech. The exception was what Washington has characterized, I think unfairly, as "Rose Garden rubbish." Those are the speeches that are *pro forma* speeches that are sometimes done by a president where the speeches, to some extent, write themselves. But for the major speeches we always had presidential guidance.

Then, whoever was the head of the speech writers would assign the speech to one of the writers; the speech would be written; it would go back and forth a few times, usually between the writer and the editor or director of the speech writers. When the director signed off on it, it would go to Bob Hartmann, who was counselor to the President and responsible for the speech writers. When Bob signed off on it, it went to the President.

Sometime later in the week we would have a second meeting with the President of about an hour and he would go over these speeches with us. (By "us" I mean it was usually Bob Hartmann, the director, me, and whoever wrote the speech.) So the speech writer always had the option of knowing what was right, what was wrong, and had a chance to fight for his or her words, and that's an extreme rarity. At any rate, the President went over every line of the speech, and if he didn't like something it would be changed on the spot, or if it called for a major rewrite, it would be redone. But essentially the President gave the speech that he wanted to give.

There were usually one or more ad-lib meetings with the President that consisted of me and the President going over the speech, usually on the plane going to an event. It was a combination of out-loud rehearsal and noodling, a fine tuning of the speech, because you can have the greatest words in type but there are some combinations of words and syllables that mortal tongues were not meant to utter. And you only find this out when you say it out loud. And so we eliminated the tongue twisters and that sort of thing.

This was pretty much the procedure that we followed up until the bicentennial speeches, and then Bob Hartmann dropped a bombshell as far as I was concerned. He said, "We're going to multiple track on the bicentennial speeches." There were six or seven of them and the President placed great emphasis and importance on them.

I was appalled; I remember getting involved in an argument. I said, "As speech writers, we all like to think of ourselves as creative people, writers. You can't throw 42 pages into a pot and pick and choose and have any of us happy." Well, that debate was won. It was won by Bob Hartmann, as it always was, and we multiple tracked. And it proved to be a marvelous idea. It was incredible. I still suggest it now for some corporate clients. It rubs writers the wrong way because when you hear a speech and you say to yourself, "Hey, that sentence is mine," it's not the same as saying to yourself, "Hey, that speech is mine." Nevertheless, we took the best thinking of everybody and as a result the bicentennial speeches were exceptionally good.

The way we did this was to call everybody into the room, including some who normally were not involved in speech writing. We told them "This is the way the speech is going to go. We are going to start with this, we are going to make these specific points, and then proceed to the close." They followed this form, and then we'd lay out all of these speeches side by side on a table, and with paste pot and scissors, we selected the best sections from each of them. It proved to be a very good idea. In fact, the acceptance speech of the nomination was put together in this form, and it got something like 65 rounds of applause because we had so many good, punchy lines that would activate and excite an audience.

As for access to the President, we never really appreciated how much access we had. Bob Hartmann, of course, was the counselor to the President—he always saw the President. I had what was known as door-knock privilege: if I had to get in to the President with something, I could get in there between appointments to talk to him for a few minutes. This hasn't been the case in all administrations.

We also always had a speech writer on the plane with the President, or a speech writer going to any event with the President. In the early days usually that was me, whether I had written the speech or not, because of the rehearsal factor. But even later on it was usually the speech writer who had written the speech who was on the plane. The value of this was most dramatically demonstrated one time when we were coming back from Los Angeles to do a speech in Ohio. Just as I got on the plane I was talking to the advance man about some of the details of the event and I suddenly realized that we had been totally misinformed about the audience. I don't know how it happened, but we thought the speech was for health care providers and actually the audience was representing organizations of health care recipients. The speech didn't make any sense for the group that we were heading for, and yet the President was going to give that speech in just four hours.

Now one of the nice things about Air Force One is that it's a flying office. We had copying machines and typewriters, and now I'm sure they have word processing machines, but we also had a phone system that maintained instant communication with Washington. So immediately I got on the phone and I explained the situation to my office—that it was the wrong speech, we can't use it. I said, "I'm going to do the start of the speech and the end of the speech, so-and-so is going to do the development of this thought and somebody else is going to do the development of that thought, and telex it back to me on the plane." Before we got off three hours later, the President had a speech that was brand new, that had been developed by his staff and coordinated by the speech writer on the plane. So it proved to be a lifesaver in that and other situations.

How much time did it take to write a speech? President Ford did 1,200 speeches and prepared remarks in two and a half years. I think it is an all-time record. We did better than a speech a day. The average amount of time that we were given to write a speech was usually too little. We were understaffed for the amount of work that we had to do. Usually we got three to four days to write a speech and that proved to be an average. Major speeches, particularly the State of the Union, always began earlier. The State of the Union Address in any administration begins to be thought about in November and is worked on constantly until delivered.

In my own experience the closest I've ever come to writing before the time the speech had to be given was on one occasion when I wrote a speech for the President on the way to the event. It was Lincoln's birthday, 1975, and I got a phone call from Terry O'Donnell, who was in charge of the President's schedule. He said that the President got a phone call from Bob Hope, a good friend, and Bob asked the President to present him with the award Hope was being given by an organization at one o'clock that same day. I asked, "What kind of an award?" and Terry said, "Well, Hope is being named Comedian of the Century." I said, "One o'clock. All right, that's not so bad. It's about ten o'clock now." He said, "Yes, but the motorcade is leaving in ten minutes for the President to go over to the Lincoln Memorial to do his Lincoln Day speech and then he's going right to the Washington Hilton. So, when are you going to do it?" At this point I grabbed a stack of five by eight cards and some felt tip pens and I ran like mad for the motorcade. I'm in the motorcade and I'm scribbling away—not really scribbling away; I'm printing away because whatever I come up with has to be legible to the President because he may not have a chance to look at it before doing it.

We show up at the Lincoln Memorial and the President is doing his speech, and I'm printing away and I realize that I'm not going to be finished before we leave for the Hilton. So I go up to the Secret Service beside the limousine and they, of course, knew who I was, and I said, "I've got to ride over with the President." Now normally this is worked out in advance. You just don't invite yourself into the presidential limousine. I have to give them all the credit in the world; they were not authorized to do this but they realized the emergency when I explained the situation and they let me in. Now the President comes down the long steps from the Lincoln Memorial and he opens the door and gives a little start because he wasn't expecting me. I said, "Please, Mr. President, it's the only way." And we now sit side by side; he's looking out the window and I'm still working away. We show up at the Washington Hilton and they open the door for the President. I said, "Please, Mr. President, one more minute," and he signals the door to be shut and he's making small talk with the Secret Service man in front and I'm finishing my last card, and off he goes. He had one quick moment in the holding room to look at the cards and he went out and did the presentation. One of the things I've always admired about President Ford is he had and has faith in his people. Until you let him down he gives you the benefit of the doubt. He figures you are going to do the job that you were hired to do. And in this case it worked out very well.

I still remember the opening line. He got out in front of this massive audience, two thousand people, and when you are giving an award to Bob Hope you can't do it in a solemn manner. President Ford started out by saying that it was an occasion that was really good news and bad news for him. He said, "The good news is that I'm here today to name my good friend Bob Hope as the Comedian of the Century. The bad news is, how am I ever going to explain this to Earl Butz?"

Let me mention one use of a speech writer that isn't being made. It's based on something that I experienced during the Ford fight for the nomination against Governor Reagan. I feel that a presidential speech writer, or speech writer anywhere, should be part of the acceptance process and they very rarely are. Usually the acceptance of a speaking engagement is determined by a scheduling department and the President—and is then presented to the speech writer. Then the speech writer has to sit down and grind out the words, and that's sometimes unfair because sometimes the words shouldn't be ground out at all.

I think back to an incident that happened in North Carolina when we had just about licked Governor Reagan for the nomination. We had won four primaries, this was the fifth, and it was generally considered that if we won North Carolina the Reagan forces would throw in the towel. We were going like a house on fire and we did three or four very good appearances. And then the President was scheduled to appear at a girls' high school to address a group of perhaps 1,800 young ladies, 14 to 18 years old. I think it was a Future Homemakers of America group. I remember looking at this and thinking, "Why have they scheduled this in the midst of a knock-down-drag-out political battle for the primary? What are we going to say to these kids?" Well, we did the obligatory mom-and-apple-pie-in-America speech and it went over surprisingly badly. The kids were quiet—they stared at the President; it got a very quiet reaction. I couldn't understand it because it was the right speech for the group, and the sort of speech that political figures have made through the years to such a group. We got trashed by the press. They pointed out that the audience stared at the President, and why would such an inept speech be given at such a point in the President's fight for the nomination? I couldn't understand it either.

A few days later I was talking to one of the advance men about it. I said I couldn't understand why the speech was scheduled, but since it was scheduled, I couldn't understand the audience's reaction because normally kids are thrilled to death to be hearing the President of the United States. He said, "You don't know what happened?" I said, "What happened? I only arrived with the presidential party." He said, "Just before the presidential party arrived, perhaps the dean of women, the principal, some school official, stood up and the place was pandemonium. Kids were screaming and yelling 'The President is coming!' and the place was jumping. When she got order she said, 'Look, this is the first and perhaps the only time in the history of this school that a President of the United States has ever come to this auditorium, and if I hear one peep out of you, you are going to hear from me about it!" And then the President of the United States walked into this thoroughly chilled auditorium. Toward the end the kids livened up a little, but it was a disaster. Regardless of that unexpected curve of the kids being told to simmer down, we should never have accepted that speech invitation at that time.

One thing that I don't know if anybody has really discussed here about working in the White House is the tension. I guess it's not considered macho to talk about the effects of tension, but after we were defeated in 1976, President Ford immediately told us that President Carter would be our leader for the next four years. "I want you to help him and his staff as much as you possibly can," and we all did. But nobody came to me, as head of the speech writers, to represent the new writing team. I didn't realize it at the time, but they had really not focused on speech writing and they had not appointed anybody. On about 15 January, five days before we were to leave, I got really steamed about it. I tried to reach Jody Powell, couldn't reach him and got Stu Eizenstat, and I put the blast on him. I said, "You know, you people are coming into this operation like you're going to run a peanut stand, and it's a lot more complicated than that. We want to help you people but when we go, there won't be anybody else around to help you. There hasn't been a Democrat in the White House in a long time that you will be able to call on. So if you want any help from the speech writing department, you'd better send somebody over."

A couple of days later Jamie Fallows shows up. Jamie was almost instantaneously, perhaps on my phone call, made head of the speech writers. He came over and we talked for about an hour. Finally Jamie stood up and said, "Is there anything else you could tell me?" I thought to myself, "If I, coming in two and a half years earlier, had been told by anybody that I was going to experience more tension and anxiety than I ever realized existed on this planet, I would have thought to myself, 'Good heavens, I've been in show business all my life; I've worked under tension, I know what tension is.'" But you don't know what tension is until you begin to work in the White House. Milton Friedman, President Ford's senior speech writer, always characterized it as part of the air there, it's fed in by the air conditioning. Tension is with you at all times, and it's very hard to be a free spirit.

A couple of days after I came to the White House we went to a reception for the press at the White House. This was about 12 days after President Ford had assumed office. Milt Friedman introduced me to a reporter as a new speech writer and the reporter said, "How many speech writers are there now in the White House?" I don't know what prompted me to say this. I turned to Milt and said, "I don't know, Milt, how many are there now? Is it five or six hundred?" And immediately the pen came out. "What do you mean?" the reporter asked. I realized from that point on, you had to be on your good behavior 24 hours a day. And that tension ultimately gets to you.

The only person who didn't seem to be very much affected by it was President Ford. I saw myself crumble; I saw my colleagues crumble; but he bore up under it amazingly well. And yet I feel this tension has to reach any president. What comes to my mind when I hear of tension is, for example, sitting in the Oval Office working over speeches in a rather relaxed scene, and suddenly the buzzer rings and it is so-and-so who wants to come into the meeting because there is a problem. Well, you don't interrupt a presidential meeting unless it is something quite important, so Secretary of State Kissinger might come in, and the speech writers are sitting there while Kissinger outlines some problem of considerable importance. We are all watching Kissinger and then as soon as the problem is presented, all eyes, like a moving picture camera, pan to and focus on the President. The common thought is, "Mr. President, how do we proceed?" I never saw any evidence of President Ford feeling this tension, but I feel that he must have.

I'm going to say something on presidential humor and then I am going to hold for questions. President Ford has a good natural sense of humor. He likes to use humor. President Ford used humor a great deal in his speeches and in his relationships with others—and that's particularly important when you are President of the United States. The more powerful you are in a position—if you are a CEO in a major corporation or you are the President of the United States—the more important it is that you eliminate the emotional and psychological gap between you and the audience. If you are President of the United States, you are standing up at a lectern, high above the audience. The Secret Service always leaves a certain amount of space between the first seat and the president as a reaction space, and the last thing a president or a CEO of a large corporation wants is to have that gap. And so it is very important that a president start off a speech with humor that reaches out and communicates on an emotional level with that audience.

I'll give you one example of how President Ford did it. The President had accepted a speech at the University of Notre Dame on 17 March, on St. Patrick's Day in 1975. Many of his advisers in the White House felt that he shouldn't do the speech. There was a serious recession going on; there was still a great deal of hard feeling about the President's pardon of Richard Nixon; the Vietnam situation was still a high visibility problem; and there had been a great deal of feeling in the White House that a college campus was the last place that a president should go at that point. There was some fear of actual violence. It was not altogether unjustified, because I still remember one of the last bits of campaigning President Ford did in October of 1974, for congressional candidates. The presidential party was actually chased into the field house of the University of Vermont. I was one of the last people to get in before the door was slammed, and it was touch and go. There was a crowd of maybe 200 or 300 kids. I don't think they meant any violence to the President, but they were moving in on him and started to run toward him and we had just this thin phalanx of Secret Service. It could have been a very bad scene. That sort of thing is what we were concerned about.

But the President wanted to do the speech and said that he was going to do the speech. The problem was how could we reach out in this field house, talking to 14,000 students, 1,000 faculty, and make instant communication with the group? As always, the President wanted to use humor. I spent a much more than normal amount of time working on jokes, and I came up with perhaps 30 possibilities and finally decided on just a few. We did an obligatory St. Patrick's Day joke and then the one that I figured would do the trick is this joke, which was written for President Ford at the University of Notre Dame. This is the joke as written:

As your next door neighbor from Michigan, I've always been impressed by the outstanding record of the students of the University of Notre Dame. You've always been leaders in academic achievement, in social concerns, in sports prowess. And now, once again, you are blazing new paths in the development of new concepts in mass transportation. Some communities have the monorail, some have the subway, Notre Dame has the quickie.

Now I see you are underwhelmed. So let me just play a tape of the President doing this joke at the University of Notre Dame, and I'm going to let the audience reaction go to its limit, and then make a few comments concerning it. [Tape of audience laughter and applause]. That reaction was 28 seconds long. The average big joke in show business runs four or five seconds. The place exploded; kids were standing on their chairs, yelling, screaming, laughing, pandemonium! Now, what was that all about?

In South Bend, Indiana, where of course the University of Notre Dame is, the drinking age is 21 years or over. In Michigan, just nine miles, the drinking age at that time was 18 years or over. So the big problem that the students had at the University of Notre Dame was how to get up to Michigan, those nine miles, to do some weekend drinking. And how did they solve it? They bought themselves a bus, and what did they call the bus? The quickie. It had the four elements of what I call a relevant demand-laugh joke.

The first element was surprise. When the President started to go into that long, laborious buildup, and calculatedly so, the kids were convinced they were going to get another long, dull, boring, "the future is yours" pap, baloney speech that they get at most every commencement exercise. You could see their eyes starting to glaze. Worse—halfway through that build, if you listened to the tape very carefully, you would hear that one of the kids yelled out "Bull!" Actually, I think it was a two-syllable word. There was laughter around it which indicated that there was potential hostility in that audience. But at the point where the President hit the quickie, they were completely caught off guard. So surprise is a big factor.

Relevance is another big factor. I saw a videotape of the President doing this, and when the place went up for grabs, they had maybe 40 or 50 of the faculty sitting in seats in back of the President on this raised platform, and one of the faculty leaned over and whispered something to one of the professors and the professor looked back and shrugged. What was obviously happening was that the faculty member was saying "What's a quickie?" And the professor was saying, "I don't know." But the President knew, and the kids knew, and the kids knew the President knew, and at that moment the President and the kids were as one. Now that doesn't mean that for the rest of the speech the kids were going to buy, just sop up, everything the President said. But at that point or at any point during the speech, if somebody was going to challenge the President or heckle the President, you could bet that the kids wouldn't stand for it: "Hey, that's my friend, the President. You hear him out."

I'm always asked how many jokes a CEO or a president should use. Well, I had a feeling that this was either going to be a tremendous success or a tremendous bomb. The President is a gutsy performer, a gutsy speaker. If he had gone through that whole build and then hit that punch line and stopped, and we hadn't been right about the impact of the quickie, you can bet that we would have had a sidebar in the paper the next day, saying the President told a joke that went into the ground. But it was so effective that in the South Bend paper the next day on the front page there was a box right in the middle of the page, outlining the quickie joke. So it had been enormously successful.

Normally, I feel you do one big joke and get out, but I also felt that, if we were right about this joke, we could take advantage of what in show business is called a roll. Once you get the audience on your side you can almost recite the telephone book and they'll enjoy it. And that was so in this case.

The President did one more joke and I'll just play it for you now and then I'll quit. The audience had come over to the President's side so strongly that they laughed on three straight lines: "This has been a most exciting day. As we were getting off the plane at the county airport [laughter] a rather amazing thing happened. [laughter] Somebody asked me how to get to the campus of the University of Notre Dame. [laughter] What made it so amazing—it was Father Hesburgh." [long and loud laughter]

So I've burned up an hour of extemporaneous no-notes remarks but perhaps I can answer some specific questions you might have.

QUESTION: I would like to ask about the speech writing coordination between Senator Dole and President Ford during the fight for the nomination in 1976. Senator Dole relied heavily on humor, but it seemed to me that it kind of backfired. Were the speeches coordinated with the President's speeches? Did your department have anything to do with his?

MR. ORBEN: Well, certainly the humor wasn't coordinated. Bob Dole is a very witty man, and at that point I think he was on his own as far as humor was concerned. In those days he got labeled as the hatchet man, and that's kind of unfortunate because he likes to use humor and sometimes it is a rather acerbic humor. On the other hand, thanks to his wife, Elizabeth, he has now become much more mellow. He still uses humor a great deal, but it is more of the type of humor that President Ford used. I always characterize it as arm-around-the-shoulder humor. It is more affectionate humor than biting humor. Senator Dole has moved in that direction.

As far as coordination is concerned, there was precious little. The Dole writers knew the themes, and we knew the themes, and I frankly don't remember much in the way of either conferring or collaborating with them. They pretty much went their own way.

Once somebody becomes vice president of the United States, there is usually a substantial gap in communication between the staffs, not necessarily between the president and vice president. I would guess that George Bush's staff has precious little to do with the White House. When Ford was vice president, there was precious little communication between the vice presidential staff and the president's staff, and maybe that was good.

COMMENT: I asked that because I felt that Senator Dole's abrasiveness really was a hindrance to the election of Ford, and that may be an important thing.

MR. ORBEN: I personally wouldn't ascribe that much importance to it. But he became aware of the fact that it was not creating an appealing personality for himself, and I think he has since learned that lesson.

QUESTION: To go back to your quickie, are there certain advanced methods that you use in order to be wired into the group that you are going to be addressing in order to use humor that is that pinpointed to the audience? You said that the faculty members did not know what a quickie was. How do you get that information?

MR. ORBEN: At the present time, one of my ways of making a living is giving seminars and workshops on communication to corporate speech writers. I spend a lot of time on the procedures to be followed and it takes a lot of time to describe them adequately, but I'll try to shorten it to a few minutes.

In the old days when Bob Hope had a radio show, he would sometimes do remotes. For example, he would come to Charlottesville and do a radio show here. Before he showed up, three or four days in advance, two writers would show up and they would talk to as many people as possible. They'd find out where the hangouts were and how the football team was doing, and all the inside things that you would kid about among yourselves. And then, with that information, they would write local jokes.

How did the quickie come about? Well, my procedure always was: first, you start with calling the people you have on the list as being responsible for the event, members of the faculty and such. I always used to point out that the President liked to start off with some lightness. And what are you kidding each other about in South Bend, Indiana? And you can count on the reaction being, "Oh, there's nothing funny around here." You can count on that. But you can't quit there; you've got to keep talking. And so I say, "How about the football team?" and that usually gets either comments on how good or bad they're doing. You keep asking questions.

On this special occasion I went through most of the faculty advisers that I had on the list, and I was getting nowhere. Then I called some of the student leaders, and in a way they are almost as bad as the faculty because the student leaders are not going to make any mistakes. They are going for chancellor or president, so they are not going to tell you anything that is going to get them into trouble. So I went through the whole bit without any success. Then I called a student who was more of a free spirit and he told me about the mystery meat in the school cafeteria, and every school has the mystery meat, so you don't want to go with that sort of cliché subject. But then he said, "Well, there is the quickie," and he giggled. So I wrote down the quickie. I said, "What's the quickie?" and he told me it's the bus that they bought. I said, "That doesn't have a double meaning, does it?" My name isn't exactly Neil Simon, but it is known somewhat. I was always afraid of some smart aleck kid setting me up. He said, "No, no, it's the bus." So I thanked him.

And now I call up another student and we go through the mystery meat and the football team and all the rest. He never mentions the quickie. And finally at the end of all this, I said, "Have you heard of something called the quickie?" and he giggled. I said, "What is it?" and he said, "It's the bus," and once again, "This doesn't have a double meaning, does it?" and he said, "No." So I put a check mark beside the quickie.

Now I call a third student and we go through the whole drill again, the mystery meat, and he never mentioned the quickie but as soon as I mentioned the quickie, he laughed. So I knew what the subject was. And when you have that magic type word, then the whole idea in writing a joke about it is how do you get to the quickie so that the quickie is the very last word of the very last sentence? You do that by just picking up on what it is—it's a transportation mode—and then you construct the whole thing as a description of normal modes of transportation and you end with the quickie.

This incident also illustrates the value of access to the President. If I didn't have a one-to-one personal relationship with President Ford, the quickie never would have been done, because if I were working in the bowels of the Old Executive Office Building, sending up material through the chain of command, some hero, halfway up the staffing chain, would have looked at it and said, "The quickie—sounds dirty" and he would have eliminated it and I never would have known who did me in. Interestingly enough, when we reviewed the speech in the Oval Office, somebody raised this point, that quickie has several meanings. Is it possible that this would be construed as a dirty joke? And the President looked over at me and said, "What do you think?" I told him the whole drill that I had just gone through and I said, "To my knowledge there is no double meaning to it. It just means the bus," and we never had any problem with it. All it did mean was the bus.

NARRATOR: Is there any way that President Ford could have turned around this ridicule of him that the best athlete in the history of the presidency seemed to be clumsy?

MR ORBEN: That really irritated me, this question of his being called clumsy or inept. Here's the most athletic president we have had in this century. The man was captain of the University of Michigan football team; he was offered two spots on professional football teams; he played in the East-West Shrine game, which is an all-star game. He was a center when the quarterback didn't take the ball out of your hands; he had to pass it back to the quarterback who was on the run and lead the quarterback so that he didn't have to break stride.

One of the interesting things about President Ford at the White House is that women used to love to dance with him because he was so agile and such a good dancer. So to have him criticized for being clumsy used to infuriate me. If it infuriated him as well, he never said so.

I had an ongoing battle with some of the White House people about this. The only way you can combat negative image humor is with more humor. If somebody did a joke—Chevy Chase would joke about it every week—and you would try to rebut it by saying, "Oh, you don't understand, he was captain of the football team" and all that—you look dull. "What's the matter, can't you take a joke?" is the answer to that sort of rebuttal. The only way we could have overcome that image battle would have been by the use of humor. I had many discussions, if not arguments, at the White House with others who felt we should ignore it. We should look the other way or we should get mad. Well, that's nonproductive. I won a few battles; I lost most. But we did win a few.

When President Ford went to Japan there was a picture taken of him shaking hands with either the emperor or the prime minister, and the President had on—I don't know where he got them—the world's shortest pair of striped pants. When he bent over to shake hands they came half way up to his knees, and newspapers ran this picture prominently. So the President came back from the Japanese trip—I wasn't on that trip—and he called me into the Oval Office right away and said, "Did you see that picture?" Never one to put my career on the line, I said, "What picture?" He smiled and said, "You know what picture." He said, "We've got to have some fun with that." And that night he had a speech to do at a "Scouter of the Year" banquet in Washington. So he opened his speech that night with: "They say once a Scout always a Scout, and I can tell you from my own experience that is true. After all these years I still love the outdoors. I still know how to cook for myself, at least breakfast. And as anyone who saw those pictures of me in Japan will know, on occasion I still go around in short pants." That made all three networks, and at that point all the cartoons and all the kidding about the short pants stopped. I felt that if we had done the same thing about the clumsiness issue it would have stopped.

One quick example of that: what started this image role were two very unfair, unkind and untrue remarks by Lyndon Johnson about Congressman Ford when he was minority leader. One was he played football too long without a helmet; the other was that he couldn't chew gum and walk at the same time. Actually Johnson's original quote was a little more pungent than that, but that's the way it usually appears.

At any rate, one time President Ford went up to Yale University for the Yale Law School's Sesquicentennial Convocation, and he started off his speech by saying, "It's a great pleasure to be here at the Yale Law School's Sesquicentennial Convocation, and I defy anyone to say that and chew gum at the same time." And again it made all three networks. The message was, "Yes, I know what's being said and I feel so confident in myself that even I can make jokes about it." If he had done more along those lines, I think we would have been better off.

QUESTION: Were you ever able to arrange for the speech department to be in on the scheduling sessions so you'd have some input?

MR. ORBEN: Not really. I came to the conclusion that this would have been a good thing after the North Carolina event, because that was the first occasion we really suffered from. There were speeches that you would write and say, "Why are we doing this?" But it wasn't a problem. The North Carolina event was a problem. By that time we were in a hard and no-holds-barred struggle for the nomination with Governor Reagan and we were all sort of hanging on by the fingernails just trying to get the product out. But I think that sort of judgment from the speech writers should be part of the speech writing process.

QUESTION: One of the most difficult acts to do well is to deliver a written speech as if it were from the heart. Did you work with Ford or other speech writers on the delivery process?

MR. ORBEN: It's a two-fold problem: the speech has to be constructed in such a way that it comes across as conversation more than essay. Beyond that there was some amount of coaching, but the President has a warm personality and, left to his own resources, does the right thing. I've always regretted very much that I wasn't a part of the preparation for the debates. It was interesting that at the very first debate, if you recall, something went wrong with a component of the sound system and for 26 incredible minutes you had the President of the United States and Governor Carter standing in back of these lecterns waiting for the sound to come on. That was characterized at the time as looking like two fellows in a tailor shop waiting for their pants to be given back. They spent 26 minutes immobilized in front of a huge national audience.

I have always felt that President Ford, a very natural person, after a few minutes would normally have said, "Well, this is absurd" and smiled and come down and sat on the thrust of the stage and made small talk with the audience and he would have looked marvelous; instead they both stood up there like mannequins in a store window and they both looked bad. I think they both had probably been so mesmerized by staff with the importance of this debate and not to do anything wrong, and so they didn't do anything natural either, and that was unfortunate.

QUESTION: You sounded as if you use humor at the beginning of a speech. Do you steer clear of it at the end?

MR. ORBEN: No, in fact we came up with one of the best endings for a bicentennial speech. It was for a speech given on 3 July at the Kennedy Center. The President closed by saying:

> Two hundred years ago today, John Adams wrote his wonderful wife, Abigail, that he expected the glorious anniversary of independence to be observed down through the ages 'with shows, games, sports, guns, bells, bonfires, and illuminations from one end of this continent to the other.' So break out the flags, strike up the band, light up the skies, let the whole wide world know that the United States of America is about to have another happy birthday, going strong at 200, and in the words of the immortal Al Jolson, 'You ain't seen nuthin' yet!'

And that Jolson quote made me feel kind of sheepish because I had been in show business all of my life and it was someone from the academic community who thought of it. Oh, well—it was a marvelous ending to the speech and set just the right tone for the entire event.

I'll give you an example of one of the problems with humor. If the speaker, president, CEO, or anybody, uses humor in the middle of a speech, if you are into heavy stuff and suddenly you go into humor, you have to signal to the audience that now it is fun time because if you don't, it may happen so fast the audience might not immediately recognize it as humor. And worse, what will happen is the audience may react a couple of sentences later when you are back into the heavy thoughts again. This is the best example I can give you: President Ford went to Cincinnati to dedicate an environmental office building and it was an extraordinarily hot day. It was 96 degrees; it was an outdoor event; the audience was hot and uncomfortable. In the middle of the speech he was talking about what our administration had done to clean up the environment. He gave a few examples and finally said, "And as a result of our efforts, fish have once again been seen in the upper reaches of the Hudson River." He said, "They cough a lot but they're there."

When we went over the speech on the plane, I pointed out that the joke came out of the blue. I said, "What you really have to do is at the point where you state that fish have once again been seen in the Hudson River—you've got to smile and sort of kick the dust a little and then do the line. If you don't, it's going to come too fast." It was a hot day, he was perspiring, the audience was perspiring, and he sailed right through it. And the joke itself got next to nothing. But then a sentence and a half later, people started thinking about it and he got a big laugh at that point. President Ford has always been very aware of audience, and as soon as he heard that laugh, he stopped, laughed along with them, and then picked up the beginning of the sentence. That's always the danger if you drop humor into the middle of the speech; you better make sure that the audience knows it's fun time.

NARRATOR: I'm sure that others have had the same thought I have. If the president of a university or any of our leaders want to get any help with the leavening effect of good humor and goodwill, the first person they ought to turn to is Bob Orben. Thank you very much.

CHAPTER 4

Carter's
Political Rhetoric

GADDIS SMITH

NARRATOR: One of Gaddis Smith's major contributions has been the education of a stream of graduate students who have gone on to become educational leaders. One of his students recently won the Porter Prize, Yales's most distinguished prize for the best Ph.D. dissertation in humanities, arts, and sciences at Yale.

Professor Smith's own work is in the field of American maritime and diplomatic history. All of us in international relations have benefitted enormously from his contributions in the field of diplomatic history.

He is the author of the book *Morality, Reason and Power*. Its value lies not only in its reporting of what happened in the Carter administration, but also in its framing of issues and problems in terms of a coherent set of ideas against which he undertakes to judge the Carter presidency. He is the author of an earlier book on Dean Acheson as secretary of state, as well as a history of wartime diplomatic relations presented in the tradition of his mentor, Samuel Flagg Bemis. Professor Bemis was one of the earlier great figures in the field of diplomatic history.

Gaddis Smith was born in New Jersey, took both his undergraduate and graduate degrees at Yale, taught for three years at Duke University, returned to Yale, and has been there ever since. He has been chairman of the History Department and master of Pearson College, but fortunately for his students and for all of us, he has also enriched our understanding of the field of diplomatic history through scholarly writings.

PROFESSOR SMITH: When Professor Thompson asked me to discuss Jimmy Carter's rhetoric, I was delighted to accept, but rhetoric as such is not a subject on which I have focused in the past. I've seen it as an essential part of government, but I do not pretend to be an authority on rhetoric in a technical sense. I'd like to start by giving you my working description of what it means to study a president's rhetoric, and then describe some standards that we might apply to presidential rhetoric generally before going into Jimmy Carter's rhetoric itself.

Rhetoric in its broadest meaning is the use of words in discourse. That's too broad for our purposes, though, and so I propose that Carter's public use of words, those delivered orally in person while he was President, be used to define the texts that we will study. This might be a bit arbitrary since he undoubtedly used a good deal of rhetoric in private dealings with the National Security Council or in secret sessions with foreign ministers, but we don't have the transcripts yet for use of that rhetoric. There is also rhetoric in private written communications but, again, the vast bulk of President Carter's papers are not yet open for historians. We also have second-hand reports of what Carter said in situations where his words were not recorded, but these sources are problematic, and I'm going to exclude those. We also have purely written texts, such as annual budget messages which go on sometimes for hundreds of pages. These texts weren't written by the President himself, and so we can exclude them. We will also, for convenience sake, exclude texts prepared before he was

President—the campaign speeches of 1976, for example—or things written since he stepped down from the presidency—his memoirs and several other books.

There is always a problem of authorship, and this is a problem for anyone studying a president. We all know that presidents have large staffs of speech writers and that their public statements are often an amalgam of material presented by different Cabinet agencies and departments, and then worked over by the speech writers.

It is possible when all of the archives are open to trace out exactly which sentence and which paragraph came where and to know exactly how a speech was changed by speech writers and then by the president. But we don't yet have full access to that material for President Carter, and it is an enormous task to reconstruct that kind of literary history for every speech. I haven't done that kind of reconstruction, so I'm going to assume that if Jimmy Carter said it personally, then that's his rhetoric. He chose to say those words even though they may literally have been written, in many cases, by other people. Indeed, if we excluded from a study of presidential rhetoric every word that was produced by somebody else, we would have Swiss cheese that was all hole and no cheese.

The source of the material that I'm using for my remarks is the familiar volume called *The Public Papers of the President*. For Jimmy Carter they are the green and blue volumes. Everyone who has dealt with American presidencies in the recent 20th century knows those invaluable volumes.

Now what is it that we want to study about presidential rhetoric? That's a much more complex question than to ask simply what the texts are for the rhetoric. We certainly do not want to engage in a purely literary analysis, like graduate students in literature trying to find something new to say about Shakespeare. We don't want to concentrate on Carter's use of the conjunction in his State of the Union addresses or gastronomical metaphors in the press conference. We are concerned with rhetoric as part of political persuasion.

The best modern book on rhetoric is *Modern Rhetoric* by Brooks and Warren, and they say that there are four elements to the art of rhetoric: *Argument*, which attempts to persuade people; *exposition*, which attempts to explain and inform; *description*, which attempts to make the listener or the reader see and feel a situation; and *narration*, which tries to show what happened and why. For our purposes, the first element, argument, is preeminent because that is what political rhetoric is all about. Political rhetoric uses the other elements— exposition, description, and narration—but they are servants to the principal purpose of argument.

The next question concerns what standards of judgment we should apply to Carter's rhetoric as argument. We cannot divorce ourselves from the larger political context or from the degree to which the President's goals were achieved or not. But we don't want to maintain the position that good rhetoric is that which works, or that rhetoric which doesn't work is bad rhetoric. For that would be rather reductionist, since we know that there are so many other factors which will determine whether a bill passes or a treaty is confirmed, or whether the Democratic party wins or loses an election. There are many other factors at work, and we must recognize that rhetoric is only one element.

An additional complexity flows from the many different audiences which a president especially seeks to influence. Let's take a nonpresidential and rather simple example. If Knute Rockne is in the locker room before the big game, and he exhorts the team to "win one for the Gipper," and the team goes out and wins, then we immediately know what the rhetoric was and who the audience was: the team. There wasn't any other audience at the time. We know the purpose, and the outcome is easy to assess. We can determine it quantitatively by the final score.

But how many different audiences and purposes are there for a president in a State of the Union address? In Carter's case, consider the State of the Union address in January 1980, which dealt somewhat with the hostage crisis in

Iran and even more with the Soviet invasion of Afghanistan. In that address there were layers upon layers of audience, both domestic and international. We as historians are part of the audience, especially in dealing with someone as recent as Jimmy Carter. I think everyone in our audience here at the Miller Center was an adult during the Carter administration. We were part of the original audience just as we are part of the historical audience now. We have our own values and our prejudices. We reacted at the time to what Carter said, and if we are now trying to be historians, the memory of how we reacted will affect our judgment. Our memory, in fact, may not be accurate, but what we think we remember affects our current opinions.

On that point, let me confess my own bias right now, because we all have biases. I respected and admired Jimmy Carter's integrity and his goals when he was President, and I respect and admire the way he has conducted himself since his retirement from the White House, but I cannot call him an effective president. Much of his difficulty can be attributed to bad luck due to circumstances beyond his control, but much of it can also be attributed to his own failings, including his failings of rhetoric. My judgment on his rhetoric is harsh, as you will see in a moment, but it is also sad because I think the rhetoric was being employed in a good cause. My judgment is also quite subjective. It draws on my own taste in rhetorical techniques, my own sense of the context of what Carter was trying to achieve, and my own comparisons of Carter's rhetoric with that of other presidents.

A moment ago I dismissed the usefulness of any purely literary analysis, but literary analysis in the sense of how words are used must be employed to some degree. I must also give you two disclaimers. First, I have not interviewed Mr. Carter or any of his aides about the subject of rhetoric. I cannot say how much of Carter's rhetorical style was deliberate and calculated, and how much of it was inadvertent. The other disclaimer is that being a neophyte in the formal subject of rhetoric, I've not researched the professional journals of speech and communication on this topic. My hunch is that there probably is already a body of literature on Carter's rhetoric by the professional students of rhetoric and the communication arts; there may even be a doctoral dissertation or two. I haven't read that material; perhaps I will at some point, but I haven't done it yet.

Jimmy Carter was a talking president; he spoke on an extraordinary number of occasions. There were news conferences twice a week during the first two years of the presidency. After midterm in 1979, however, as both domestic and international crises mounted, he reduced the number of news conferences. But before that time, there were actually call-in shows where you could dial an 800 number and have a one in a million chance to put a question over the telephone to Jimmy Carter. There were town meetings throughout the United States and abroad. One of the most interesting ones that I came upon was a session in Shimoda, Japan. There were informal question and answer sessions with all manner of groups. I haven't done a quantitative comparison, but I suspect Jimmy Carter may have had more of his spoken words recorded in the four years that he was President than any other president in our history. And there certainly wasn't any of this shouting over the clatter of the helicopter with Jimmy Carter.

Despite the quantity and variety of his public communication, there is a sameness to his rhetoric. He doesn't seem to alter the way he uses words to meet the audience or the circumstances. He spoke as if the audience for Jimmy Carter was Jimmy Carter, and I'm going to emphasize this theme. There is a very personal quality to his rhetoric, a constant reference back to his own life and his own experience. Whether this is deliberate or self-conscious, I don't know. He was not a widely read or traveled man, and his illustrations, his references, and his comparisons were drawn very largely from his own life.

I have a question that I'm going to put to this audience: who was the first person mentioned by name by President

Jimmy Carter within seconds of his taking the oath for President?

QUESTION: Wasn't it his daughter?

PROFESSOR SMITH: No, it was Julia Coleman, who was his high school English teacher. He refers to her in the very beginning of his inaugural address as someone who had a great impact on his life by teaching him spiritual values.

In the conduct of his term of office, a president has to mention thousands of individuals. He presents people, nominates people for office, and frequently has to refer to congressmen, senators, foreign leaders, his staff, and his family. I am struck with how few individuals, except for those that he has to mention in an official way, were quoted or mentioned in the whole body of Jimmy Carter's rhetoric. There were a few biblical figures and biblical quotations, and he did cite Martin Luther King, Reinhold Niebuhr, and Paul Tillich by name; he mentioned other presidents only rarely. Sometimes he used rhetoric which is reminiscent of other presidents, especially Woodrow Wilson, but seldom did he mention Wilson by name. There is indeed a thinness, a poverty of historical and literary references in his discourse.

Perhaps his emphasis on himself was calculated as part of an effort to present himself as a president of the people. He was drawing strength and wisdom from the people, people just like himself, demonstrating that in America any person, from a background no matter how obscure, could become president. (That's a paraphrase of a remark that he made often about himself.)

I sense that this self-reference was more than deliberate calculation, that it reflected a fundamental loneliness in the man, an introversion, an uneasiness in applying to the role of government the experience of others with whom he was not intimately connected. I believe he was speaking truthfully when he told a group in 1979 that his rural childhood near Plains, Georgia, had been the happiest time of his life. He said something like this to that group, "When I am now in the White House in Washington, my greatest hunger is to be alone, away from the security officers, away from the press, and to be in the fields and woods again."

As a teacher and adviser to students, I, like any teacher concerned with writing, constantly harp on the importance of the lead paragraph and the lead sentence within each paragraph. Whether it is a newspaper story, a State of the Union address, or an inaugural address, it is that first sentence and that first paragraph that will have the biggest impact.

In that context I find it extraordinary that so many of Carter's leads refer to himself directly or implicitly. There is his reference to Julia Coleman and her impact on Carter at the very beginning of his inaugural. There is the famous spiritual crisis speech of 1979 known as the "malaise speech" (although he did not in fact use the word "malaise" in that speech). That speech begins with these words: "This is a special night for me. Exactly three years ago on 15 July 1976, I accepted the nomination of my party to run for president of the United States." One could be cynical about this; who cared that his nomination was exactly three years before? And why begin the speech with that, which was certainly one of the most important speeches, he thought, in his whole life? In the opening sentence of the 1980 State of the Union address, another very important address, there is an implicit self-reference: "These last few months have not been an easy time for any of us." It refers to himself: the "us" is almost the royal "we," I think, in that circumstance.

The spiritual crisis speech is one of the most interesting of all of Carter's statements. The particular substantive problem in that summer of 1979 was the energy crisis, and Carter tied that crisis to his most oft-repeated idea, that the fundamental issue was the spiritual health of the people. At the beginning of his presidency he continued to use the theme that had been very important in his campaign, which was that the spiritual health of the American people was rock solid.

GADDIS SMITH 85

He said that he had enormous confidence in the American spirit, and that he was drawing his own strength from it. He promised a government as good as the people.

There was also a contradictory claim at the same time; Jimmy Carter believed that Watergate and Vietnam indicated that there was a lack of spiritual health and that now somehow there would be a rebirth, which he would lead. So just two years after his inauguration, he spoke grimly of

> a crisis that strikes at the very heart and soul of
> our national will. We can see this crisis in the
> growing doubt about the meaning of our own lives,
> and in the loss of a unity of purpose for our nation.
> The erosion of our confidence in the future is
> threatening to destroy the social and political fabric
> of America.

You will recall, I am sure, the immediate circumstances of that speech. He originally had intended to address the nation on the energy problem early in July, but his speech was canceled at the last minute. He retreated to Camp David, and for ten days invited to join him—as he said himself—people from every segment of society: business and labor, teachers and preachers, governors, mayors, and private citizens. They were to tell him what was wrong. He filled a huge notebook in his own handwriting with their comments, and he quoted quite a bit of this in his speech. I'll just give you a sampling of the quotes from these other people: "You don't see the people enough anymore." "Some of your Cabinet members don't seem loyal." "I feel so far from government. I feel like ordinary people are excluded from political power." "Mr. President, we are confronted with a moral, spiritual crisis."

I would be interested to hear how any of you reacted to that speech. I recall that I myself did not feel that this alleged spiritual crisis was within me. I didn't feel a spiritual crisis, nor did I sense it was really widespread throughout the nation. Instead, I interpreted the speech as self-revelation; I sensed that Carter was talking much more about himself than about any objective reality in the nation. I feared that Carter was undergoing a crisis, and it did not enhance my own confidence in him at the time.

This brings me to the question of what quality it is which inspires confidence in a president's audience and constituents. I've been searching for a single word to describe it, and I've come up with "serenity." Although I have some problems with that word, I'm going to use "serenity." "Serenity" is sort of a Pennsylvania Avenue version of "the right stuff."

In his fireside chat on 2 February 1977, his first address of that kind, Carter said: "I have spent a lot of time deciding how I can be a good president." I think that was probably true, but it was bad rhetoric. Someone once said that FDR never had to think about what it meant to be President: he *was* President. Most importantly, he was serene in his own identity. One sensed that no matter how serious the crisis—the Japanese attack on Pearl Harbor or the terrible economic crisis of the Great Depression—FDR's own personal stability was not at risk. This calm quality that I have in mind is not the same as passivity by any means, because serenity can be the companion of enormous activity, energy, and commitment. Thinking of 20th century presidents, I would say that Theodore Roosevelt had it, as well as Franklin Roosevelt. Wilson had it through 1918, and then lost it very emphatically. Eisenhower had it and so did Kennedy. Lyndon Johnson had some of it. Hoover lacked it as did Nixon, Ford, Harding, and Coolidge. I would rank Truman as somewhat neutral on this. Whatever you think of Reagan, he had serenity. Carter was decidedly without it.

I, as well as virtually everyone who has written on the foreign policy of the Carter administration, have commented on its schizophrenic nature, torn between Secretary of State Vance's efforts to solve conflict through negotiation; Zbigniew Brzezinski's passion to change Soviet behavior by threat, intimidation, and the infliction of pain; and Carter's own moral sense. Both Vance and Brzezinski had quite different approaches, and they both appear in Carter's speeches. Carter's failure to recognize the tension in these two approaches at times led to an awkwardness that bordered on incoherence. I'm not saying that he should have opted entirely for one or the other because the tension is there; it is real, but I think it has to be confronted and explained.

The confusion in policy and the confusion in rhetoric were much the same thing. Indeed, I think the problem of the way in which his speeches were put together was that sometimes these conflicts appear within the same speech. This confusion found expression in Carter's shifting invocation of historical meaning, rare though the invocation of history was. It also found expression in his unfortunate penchant for exaggeration, which is characteristic of his rhetoric.

In his Notre Dame speech of May 1977, which came closer than any other early statement to expressing his personal vision of a better world, Carter made the famous declaration that, "Being confident of our own future, we are now free of that inordinate fear of communism which once led us to embrace any dictator who joined us in that fear. For too many years we have been willing to adopt the flawed and erroneous principles of our adversaries, sometimes abandoning our own values for theirs. This approach failed with Vietnam, the best example of its intellectual and moral poverty." It is a very, very interesting passage.

Two and a half years later the Soviets intervened in Afghanistan, and Carter indulged in great exaggeration. He called that event the greatest threat to world peace since the Second World War, and then he described its relationship in history in a way that was completely different from his reading of history back in the Notre Dame speech. He said, "Since the end of the Second World War, America led other nations in meeting the challenge of Soviet power. In the 1940s we took the lead in creating the Atlantic Alliance in response to the Soviet suppression and consolidation of its East European empire. In the 1950s we helped to contain further the Soviet challenge in Korea and the Middle East. In the 1960s we met the Soviet challenges in Berlin and faced the Cuban missile crisis," and so on. There was no mention of Vietnam, and no mention of moral and intellectual poverty.

I think both of these interpretations of history have some validity, and a president with a greater historical sense could have shown how they were interrelated. But Carter, with his penchant for hyperbole, exaggeration, and oversimplification, seemed to throw out one interpretation without any trace whatsoever in order to embrace another.

Let me end on a more sympathetic note. I see Jimmy Carter as someone who tried simultaneously to think and act in several different realms. First, he was most comfortable in the lonesome, somewhat introverted role of the boy growing up near Plains, wandering in the woods and fields. He was also comfortable with a small circle of friends and family from Georgia.

As for the second realm, he was definitely uncomfortable at the level of national politics. He, like Ronald Reagan, campaigned against Washington as something alien to the true American character. But when Ronald Reagan got to Washington, he gloried in it. He triumphed and really loved the place. He may have continued to engage in anti-Washington rhetoric, but he was really in his element. Carter hated Washington, and he hated it even more at the end than at the beginning of his presidency; this shows in his rhetoric.

The third realm was that of the universal world of all mankind and of the human spirit, and Carter tried to be most truly American by seeing himself and the nation in service to all mankind, not just to the narrow interest of one nation. It is in this sense that he was the most Wilsonian of our recent presidents. This vision and the tension between the world view and the national view was eloquently expressed in Jimmy Carter's farewell address, which is my favorite. He simultaneously reaffirmed the necessity of maintaining American armed strength, while eloquently describing the consequences of nuclear war and the threat of environmental disaster. "We see our earth as it really is, a small and fragile and beautiful blue globe, the only home we have." I think that echoes both Plains and the whole world. "We see no barriers of race or religion or country." Of course, the reality was that the barriers were everywhere, but this was his vision. "We see the essential unity of our species and our planet, and with faith and common sense, that bright vision will ultimately prevail." And that, I think, was Jimmy Carter at his best, both in rhetoric and in thought.

QUESTION: Do you think that his failed rhetoric accounts for his incredibly low popularity rating with the American people—37 percent against Reagan's 67 percent? He never sold himself to the American people.

PROFESSOR SMITH: That's correct. Especially in the "spiritual crisis speech," he attacked the American people. He was basically saying that the problem here was that we were spiritually sick, that we had this spiritual crisis. That wasn't the problem; the problem was the Middle East, OPEC, and some difficulties we had in the distribution of oil. Jimmy Carter's gloominess certainly contributed to his own unpopularity. He also had a lot of very bad luck and bad timing.

COMMENT: I was interested in the popularity rating. Not only was he very low among the American people, but the American Bar Association ran a popularity rating among the lawyers, and it was just about as bad as for the American people as a whole.

PROFESSOR SMITH: As I said at the beginning, I admire him as a person and I admire his goals, but I have to rate him pretty low in terms of effectiveness.

QUESTION: Do you think his record would have been viewed differently if the hostage crisis and the oil crisis had not occurred?

PROFESSOR SMITH: Yes, I think that these issues are where you have circumstances that were in part beyond his control. I think the Soviets were the most important factor of all. The Soviets were in a period of incredibly bad leadership, which Gorbachev and almost everybody else in the Soviet Union now are recognizing. "Brezhnev" is becoming one of the dirtiest words in the Soviet rhetorical vocabulary today. This was the period when the Soviet Union was led by a succession of zombies and people who were quite literally on the edge of death. It was paralysis, rigidity of the worst sort leading to incredible Soviet blunders, in both domestic and foreign policy. The worst blunder of all was the invasion of Afghanistan, which seemed to undermine what little there was left of the more positive view that Jimmy Carter had held concerning possibilities for international cooperation. We can speculate about what might have been had Gorbachev somehow come to power in Moscow at the same time that Jimmy Carter came to power in Washington. My guess is that Jimmy Carter would have been reelected and things would have been quite different.

The hostage crisis in Iran was the end product of 30 years of American-Iranian relations. It cannot be blamed on Carter himself. There is a lot of speculation as to whether he could have handled it differently. Carter believed, and I think this is part of his moral code, that the most important issue concerning the American hostages in Iran was their lives. He would do everything possible to preserve their lives. Some of his advisers said, "No, Mr. President, there is a national interest that transcends the lives of hostages, and we basically have to affirm our strength and act quickly and immediately." Zbigniew Brzezinski, the national security adviser, wanted the United States to take military action within a few days of the taking of the hostages. It might well have killed the hostages, and Jimmy Carter might have come out with little more damage than Ronald Reagan did from the death of 243 Marines in the barracks in Beirut, but Jimmy Carter refrained from doing that. He did then authorize the rescue attempt, which failed very early on, long before the team got anywhere close to Teheran. In the end we all remember that the hostages were released within minutes of the beginning of the Reagan administration, and no lives were lost. The hostages were certainly a dark cloud that hung over the last year of Carter's presidency, though.

QUESTION: Did he actually legally change his name from James to Jimmy?

PROFESSOR SMITH: I don't know. He signs all his presidential papers Jimmy Carter rather than James Earl Carter.

QUESTION: Didn't the Camp David Accords give him a great deal of satisfaction and also elevate his image in the eyes of the American people?

PROFESSOR SMITH: I think they did. He had substantial achievements in foreign affairs, one of which, the Panama Canal Treaties, in fact hurt him politically despite being quite an achievement. He narrowly got them through the Senate, and public opinion polls pretty consistently showed that the majority of the American people were against them, but I still think it was better to have signed those treaties than not.

Camp David was an achievement. It wasn't a panacea, which we now certainly know. It ended the formal state of war between Egypt and Israel and led to the withdrawal of Israel from the Sinai, but it did not lead to the Palestinian autonomy in the occupied territories, which was envisioned in the Camp David Accords. I think Mr. Carter was suckered by the Israeli government on that one. He had much higher expectations than the reality of Israeli policy warranted. How much the accords contributed to his popularity ratings in the polls is hard to measure. It certainly wasn't enough to get him reelected. In fact he wasn't all that popular at any point with the organized American Jewish lobby. Some of them were more hard-line than the settlement in the Camp David Accords.

QUESTION: Did he rely at all on Madison Avenue for his presentation?

PROFESSOR SMITH: No.

QUESTION: To what extent do you think that his delivery had an effect upon the message that he was trying to get out?

PROFESSOR SMITH: He consciously tried to avoid the trappings of the imperial presidency. He wanted to speak in ordinary, almost conversational tones, person to person. I see why he wanted to do that and I can respect him for it, but I think it was a mistake for a president. I think in a presidential setting, especially major policy addresses, you have got to be a little bit more ceremonial than was his style. My hunch is that a lot of people said, "Well, this guy really isn't much of a leader. He's just kind of an ordinary guy; we want someone with more 'oomph' in his delivery style."

QUESTION: A lot of us thought that when Carter reached the White House, piety would become an "in" thing along the Potomac. And yet it really didn't work out that way. I am interested in the self-referencing character of so much of his discourse, and with how intimately related it is to the quality of his piety. The kind of pietism to which he was exposed and which clearly influenced him comprises a very large component of his self-referencing tendencies.
   I wonder if your suggestion is that there is indeed a schizophrenic element in this piety. On the one hand, we get the insistence on the importance of salvation, whatever

secular value that might have, while on the other we get a scolding of what the preachers would have called sin. I see his "moral crisis" speech as a kind of scolding. However, you don't see any point at which his rhetoric is significantly loaded with the biblical imagery that some of us would have expected. His vision does not seem to be either that of the Old Testament prophets or the vision of Reinhold Niebuhr. Do you see any point at which his rhetoric was decisively influenced by what he himself took to be his very deep Christian convictions?

PROFESSOR SMITH: It is interesting that in his inaugural address, after introducing Julia Coleman, he did make an explicit biblical reference. He had in the first draft of the address a passage from Chronicles. The passage that he wanted to use was: "If my people"—my people—"shall humble themselves and pray and seek my face, and turn from their wicked ways, then I will hear from Heaven and will forgive their sin and will heal their land." But at the urging of aides who claimed some listeners might think Carter was equating himself with Solomon and condemning all Americans as wicked, he chose instead Micah 6:8. The message was similar although muted: "What doth the Lord require of thee but to do justice, love mercy, and walk humbly with thy God." There are relatively few other explicit biblical references thereafter in his public discourse.

COMMENT: I do not think Carter wanted to be a Southern Baptist preacher. That doesn't get to the core of his rhetoric nearly as much as he wanted to be an engineer. It was Rickover, not Niebuhr or Tillich, that he sought to emulate. Carter, really, was all thumbs rhetorically speaking. In the South, Southern Baptist preachers have a sense of their audience.

COMMENT: Jimmy Carter did not have that. He did not have a sense of an audience, either in the old sense of his immediate face-to-face audience in a congregation or a political hall or in the modern sense that Ronald Reagan has. Reagan knows when there is a camera and a mike present; he knows that there is a great audience out there, and he knows how to play to it. Carter had neither of these skills and I think this is really the core of his failure. There are a number of books about Carter's rhetoric, but one said in effect not to just think of speeches and what is in speeches, and what appeals we use, but to think about the whole context of persuasion. I guess that gets bigger as the apparatus gets bigger.

PROFESSOR SMITH: Right, and it includes the nonverbal imagery, such as walking on Inauguration Day.

COMMENT: Hogan presents the Panama Canal as an example of a rhetorical victory for Carter. He did accomplish something important, even if most people would call it political in the narrower sense of getting the treaties through.
     There has been a problem in rhetoric which goes back to the ancients: Do you merely study technique, or do you also study the goals for which the rhetoric is used? Good technique doesn't mean good rhetoric to some people, because there is some question about what it is used for. You might say, "Well, Carter wasn't any good at it; he was all thumbs." But here was something he cared about; he did successfully persuade in a difficult situation. As you said, the treaties even succeeded against the current of popular opinion.

QUESTION: I was struck, of course, by the bad luck that President Carter had, but also I think it is an interesting speculation as to how he would have done had he been in the White House during the time of Franklin Roosevelt's first two terms. Roosevelt had the best luck you could imagine. He had the bad guys to attack, the "pirates of privilege," and he made the most of it. He got people cheering, and he got the votes. I wonder if Carter, with his religious bent or convictions, might have botched that and not done Franklin Roosevelt's job.

PROFESSOR SMITH: I don't think he would have done Franklin Roosevelt's job. Herbert Hoover hadn't been doing very well in confronting the crisis up to the time he left office. Roosevelt was a master politician in so many ways. He worked magnificently with Congress; he knew how to flatter and win the support of the members of Congress. Of course, the nation was united in a sense of a crisis with perhaps 90 percent of the people agreeing that extraordinary measures would have to be taken as a matter of national life and death in 1933. Jimmy Carter never had that, but his handling of Congress was incredibly inept in spite of the case of winning, by the narrowest of margins, the necessary Senate votes on the Panama Canal.

QUESTION: How much, if any, of the contrast between Mr. Reagan's superior rhetoric and Carter's ineffective rhetoric, do you think came out in the presidential debates in 1980?

PROFESSOR SMITH: I was biased against Reagan personally in those debates, and I must say that my reaction, I'll have to confess, was a rather elitist one. I thought, "Are the American people so dumb that they are going to be fooled by Reagan?" I wasn't for Reagan. I thought Carter handled himself pretty well in those debates. He handled himself quite well in the 1976 debates and scored a good point against Jerry Ford on the question of whether Poland was a free nation or not. Not being a professional student of rhetoric, I am still puzzled, frankly, as to the enormous appeal that Ronald Reagan has to so many people. It's almost as if it is a visceral feeling people have: This is somebody I like; this is somebody I'd like to have in my living room or sitting in the car as we drive down the highway together. This feeling seems more important than everything else.

QUESTION: It seems the malaise factor preceded Carter to the White House. I was a career employee in the foreign agriculture service, and we were made to feel guilty about everything from the parking space to the amount of gasoline that our cars used. I never went through such a grilling as those fellows put out. I don't know how Carter managed to attract some of the people around him. He himself was not doing it personally.

PROFESSOR SMITH: His close advisers were from a very narrow circle, overwhelmingly from the state of Georgia. I think you are quite right: this guilt trip that they were trying to make a lot of us feel wasn't very effective politics. Jerry Ford was in a unique and difficult, almost impossible situation: having pardoned Richard Nixon, he could not free himself of the taint of the Nixon presidency. This made for a not-to-be-repeated situation that was extraordinary, I think. Carter had bad luck once in office, but he also had had unbelievable luck in getting elected because of those circumstances.

QUESTION: Can you see any relation between Hoover's and Carter's background, both having been engineers? How might it have affected the outcome?

PROFESSOR SMITH: Any similarities would be superficial. Hoover's world experience, of course, was incredible. He had been operating before his presidency for two decades at the highest level of affairs: running the Belgian Relief and the European Relief during the First World War, being a major world figure in international mining before 1914, and then being the most important member of the Cabinet in the Harding-Coolidge years. Hoover clearly had enormous experience. Hoover was a much more authoritarian person. Although Hoover had never been in the military and though he was a Quaker, I would say he had characteristics that we often associate with military command. He commanded things to be done. When the circumstances responded to his commands, he was marvelous. When they no longer responded, as with the collapse of the world economy, he was in a pitiful condition because he didn't have political skills; he only had command skills. So I think my basic answer is no: the similarities are too superficial to be pursued too far.

NARRATOR: Whom did Carter like? Whom did Carter feel at home with?

PROFESSOR SMITH: The relationship between Jimmy and Rosalynn Carter is a very important one. Ken reminded me that I say in my book on Carter, and it is something I still hold to, that Rosalynn Carter is the most politically aware, astute, and intelligent first lady since Eleanor Roosevelt. I still hold to that.

In the realm of foreign leaders he had good relations with some Third World leaders. The closest relationship he had was with Sadat of Egypt, and he had a surprisingly good relationship with Torrijos of Panama, who was of questionable character but Carter liked him. He had very poor relations with and did not like major European figures, Helmut Schmidt being the most notable example. Schmidt did not make it easier by publicly calling Carter incompetent. I would say he had difficulty dealing with people who considered themselves more than his equal. Maybe a lot of us have that trouble.

NARRATOR: I'm sure we all now realize why Professor Gaddis Smith has such a tremendous reputation as a scholar of diplomatic history and of the Carter presidency. We thank him for being with us today.

CHAPTER 5

Ronald Reagan's Rhetoric

TOM GRISCOM

NARRATOR: The Miller Center is pleased this afternoon to welcome you to a Rotunda Lecture with Tom Griscom. In 38 brief years Tom Griscom has had an absolutely remarkable political career and is continuing aspects of it as West Professor of Communication and Public Affairs at the University of Tennessee at Chattanooga.

Tom Griscom was most recently assistant to the president for communication and planning, and in that connection his thinking drove the communications and discussions that were part of the Moscow summit as well as President Reagan's personal involvement in that summit. Many of the speeches which President Reagan gave have become memorable, notably the Moscow State University speech, and Tom Griscom had a major role in planning those speeches and editing and organizing them for delivery.

Tom Griscom began his career in Tennessee. He was a writer for the *Chattanooga News-Free Press* and gained a claim to fame in many ways. It is said that the Roundhouse, the arena in Chattanooga, should have been named after him because he endeared himself to such a wide range of people and generated interest in that activity. He was affectionately called Scoop but was also associated with the state insect at one stage when a resolution was introduced in the state legislature to honor him. As press secretary to Senator Howard Baker, he was highly regarded on Capitol Hill as the best congressional press secretary during his time on the Hill. Howard Baker used to say that Tom Griscom's press conferences were better attended than his own, and when Senator Baker went to the White House, one of the first persons to whom he turned was Tom Griscom.

It is a great privilege to have a friend from a part of the world that has been central to the life of the Miller Center—Chattanooga, Tennessee, where Burkett Miller lived and worked for many years—as our guest, Tom Griscom.

MR. GRISCOM: I always find it is best to start off by putting things in perspective. So let me tell you a little bit more about how I got to Washington and how I ended up spending ten years of my life there. I did do all the things that Ken said and I was designated at one point, if only for a few fleeting moments, as the state insect of Tennessee. I ended up being beat out by the ladybug beetle, and I guess that's appropriate. But I was the state insect for at least a short period of time.

The way I got to Washington was back in 1978. I was at the *Free Press* at that point, a political writer, and Senator Baker was up for reelection. He called me and said, "I need a press secretary. Would you come to work for me?" Now if you've been a newspaper reporter, particularly a political writer, the first thing you do is go and look through your clip file to find out what you wrote about him, because you want to make sure that if you see him that he's not going to say, "Now why did you say this about me a couple of weeks ago?" I looked through it and everything appeared to be OK, so I said, "Sure, I'd like to do that," and he said, "Why don't you come up to Huntsville, Tennessee? It's a small town about 60 miles west of Knoxville, up in the mountains, and let's talk about it." So I got in my car and drove up there from Chattanooga, and when I got there the senator said, "You know, I don't know why it took me so long to find you. I have looked now for six months. This search has taken me all across this country, and here was somebody right in my own backyard who could do the job." You can imagine me sort of swelling up with pride, saying, "My gosh, this is the minority leader of the United States Senate saying I'm the one person in this whole country who could do the job." I said, "Well, Senator, I'm really flattered that you feel that way." He said, "Let me tell you why; after traveling around I cannot find anybody other than you who could see eye to eye on the issues with me." And I thought for a minute and said to myself, "What he's telling me is that I am five feet six inches now and I'd better not grow another half-inch." If you ever saw us traveling together you always saw me standing next to Senator Baker, which made him look bigger and made me look smaller. So that is how I got to Washington and ended up at the White House. I think that helps put things in perspective.

What I want to do for a few minutes is to undertake a broad review of President Reagan, his ability to communicate, and how communication was used to portray his leadership. I don't plan to deal in detail with specific incidents, although I want to touch on them; instead I want to look at his ability to control the agenda through the use of communication. I think you have to begin by talking about what leadership is. From my point of view there are three basic elements. One is the strength of character. Are they strong individuals and can they somehow display that strength? Secondly, do they have a purpose and a direction for what they want to do? And third, can they through the first two exhibit at least some type of control and ability to dominate an agenda, to become the person who can really shape and give some direction and form to public policy? Those to me become three very critical aspects of looking at leadership and trying to define it. These are three elements that I think that most presidents bring. Maybe they don't bring all three of them, but in the case of President Reagan, I think he did. This President was also probably best at taking what I see as a communication age that was developed by TV and using TV as a medium to deliver his message and deliver it in a dominant way. So while he did not necessarily create all the techniques used to communicate, he perfected some of them and expanded on them, and then used them to his own benefit.

I think to get a sense of this President we ought to look back; let's start with President Kennedy and build up as we go through this. One is change. You hear a lot of talk right now between George Bush and Mike Dukakis about change, that the country wants change, and I think they are right. All the public opinion surveys say that it is a time for change. The question is, what type of change?

Starting with Kennedy, each president has brought a change when he came into office. When President Kennedy was elected and assumed office in 1961, it was after eight years of President Eisenhower, and so it was a time of change. President Kennedy was young and vibrant, and he had many new ideas for this country. When he was assassinated and Vice President Johnson assumed the presidency, Johnson brought more of a congressional mind-set into the office, and he used his ability to negotiate with his former colleagues in the House and Senate to try to move his agenda. However, his inability to deal with the Vietnam War, Congress, and the American people led to his downfall. Any administration, any president who cannot read and understand public attitudes and how public attitudes are important in setting policy is not going to be able to succeed. In the case of the Vietnam War, I think it was very clear that President Johnson was not able to enunciate the objectives he wanted to accomplish, and he saw a country that moved away from those objectives. Johnson then had to decide not to seek reelection.

Then came President Nixon, again a time of change. You had a country that was looking for new leadership and new direction. His main strengths were in the foreign policy area, but he had trouble dealing with power, how to control the agenda and how to deal with his adversaries in a way that he could advance the things he wanted to do.

President Ford then came in as a healer, a person who basically said, "Let's stay the course and keep the country moving ahead. Let's show that our basic constitutional guarantees work, and that this country is strong and vibrant because of those things our Founding Fathers based this country on years ago." He did not come in to offer new initiatives, and he tried not to create any new waves.

Then came President Carter. You'd had a president who had left in disgrace—a caretaker period in the presidency when the country was looking for new leadership and new direction. President Carter came in offering that. He was an untested outsider, and he basically decided he was going to take on Washington. Those of you this close to Washington understand that Washington does not react very well to that. That city decides who you are and what you are going to be, and you have to fight all your life to say, "No, I'm something else." President Carter tried to do that, and I think he was not very successful in making that happen. But I also think it is fair to say that with President Carter you got a sense of what television can do to a presidency. Here's a president caught up with hostages in Iran who decided he was not going to campaign and leave the White House. He put candles in the windows, and if you remember the TV pictures, it constantly reminded us of a president and a country being held hostage. That was the television image that created part of the political downfall for the President, and gave President Reagan a chance to offer a new direction for the office.

Change then becomes very important when you think back over the presidency. If you look at the 1988 election, you have two candidates talking about change, and I think it is a question of how you define it in 1988. Is it a change in the sense that you had one from Johnson to Nixon, from Carter to Reagan, which is basically a party change with a new set of initiatives, a new set of goals, or is it a change that says,

"*We* have been the change; let's continue that change going forward."

Let's look at President Reagan, his leadership, and the things he was able to do. Look at the words he used to describe himself: a new beginning, a new direction, offering clear, concise goals for this country to follow. Now there have been many people who would say that this President was simplistic, because he wanted to talk about balancing the budget, or cutting spending, or cutting taxes, or rebuilding our national defenses, but he could not really sit down and deal with you if you wanted to talk about the ins and outs of Superfund or other policies. Was that a strength or weakness from this President's standpoint? When he came into office, it was a strength for him because you had no doubt that this President understood who he was, the things he wanted to do, and how to communicate those things to the American people. You didn't doubt that this President also was able to stand up and say, "This is what I believe, and this is the way I want to go," and then to lead the country.

David Broder, in his book *Behind the Front Page*, wrote this about President Reagan's communication strategy:

> He was able to project his voice and his views far more widely than any other politicians. It has enhanced the power of the communicator and chief as against that of other institutions of government, particularly Congress and state and local officials. I would not strip any of these tools from the President, for communication is central to his leadership ability, and this system of government does not function well without strong presidential leadership.

Those sentences sum up what this President was able to do: to articulate a vision for America and to translate that vision into a specific set of goals to lead this country. He also did one other thing; he kept the promises that he made, not in 1980, but that he had been making basically since 1964. He did what he said he was going to do. We used to remind those people who criticized Reaganomics that this President said that he was going to try to cut spending and cut taxes, and he did what he set out to do. He didn't promise one thing and then do something else—a trait you find in many officeholders. President Reagan developed a set of themes that he felt would bring people together, what I would call a community of values.

There are a couple of other points we need to look at before we deal specifically with the President's own message and how he communicated. Keep in mind that this was the first president to serve a full eight-year term since President Eisenhower, and for many American people it is a new institution, a two-term presidency. What does it mean and how do you have to change some of your objectives from the first four years to the second four years, when you immediately become a lame duck the day after you are reelected to serve that final four-year term? That was different and something you had to recognize and deal with in shaping the presidential message.

Let's examine his inauguration speech in 1981, because I think that is really the beginning point which put into focus what this President wanted to do. I was standing out there, and the temperature was in single digits that January morning as he spoke on the west front of the Capitol. That is where this President laid out his feeling for America and the things that he wanted to accomplish. That is where he talked about Reaganomics and balancing the budget—or trying to balance it—as one of his goals. He also talked about rebuilding military strength and reinvigorating the interest that Americans have in serving in the military, and the American role in trying to shape the world and trying to make democracy once more something to be proud of and trying to use it as a governing alternative. He was also talking about how you get the government off people's back—removing regulation and allowing people to do things on their own, to be creative, and for government not to hold back but to allow people's creative genius to move forward. That is the essence of his presidential message, and those are the goals, if you think back, that he used to guide his administration. Right or wrong, whether you agree or disagree with some of the things he did, nobody in this country can ever say that Ronald Reagan did not tell them what he was going to try to do.

There was an article in the *New York Times* this morning covering a speech the President made at Georgetown University on Saturday, and I found it rather interesting. The first two or three paragraphs said that Ronald Reagan got up Saturday at a convocation and said some of the very same things that he said back in 1981. To me that is refreshing. Here is a man who has been in office almost eight years and he still remembers the core things that got him there, the things that he told this country he wanted to do, and that he still is driven by those very same things. Consistency, I think, is very important as you talk about leadership and laying out a vision or direction for this country, and let's now look at that part of it.

Communication. How do you do it? I've always looked at it from having served up on the Hill, where you've got 535 individual news makers, any one of whom wants to be on the news a given night or thinks he could be the President on a given day, versus one news maker who sits down at the other end of Pennsylvania Avenue, the President of the United States. When you work at the White House you learn very quickly that there is a big difference between one end of Pennsylvania Avenue and the other. When we were on the Hill, we were accustomed to reporters basically listening to phrases, picking up a phrase here or there, and reporting it or using it for guidance or direction. But when we got to the White House, because there is one news maker, the President, the media hangs on every syllable that you say. Sometimes you don't even have to say it; they look into your face and if you are frowning or if they ask you a question and you shrug your shoulders a little bit, then they read that as some type of communication.

You also realize the impact that one person or those who work for him can have, not just in this country but around the world. We went to our first economic summit in April of 1987, and Senator Baker had been in his office as chief of staff for about two and a half months. At that time there were questions about the Iranians using silkworm missiles supplied by China. We were standing outside the Vatican, and a reporter came up and asked, "Senator Baker, what do you think the policy of this country ought to be in dealing with Silkworm missiles?" He said, "We ought to use the Orkin strategy." I looked at him; I wasn't sure what he was getting at, but he was trying to make a joke. He was talking about Orkin the pest control company. Well, the press took that comment and within minutes put out a wire headline that said, "Chief of Staff Makes Light of Silkworm Missiles." Senator Baker came running up and said, "What did I do wrong? I always talk this way; don't they know I was kidding?" That's the difference between being at the White House and being a member of Congress. The press is waiting for whatever it is that you say because you replace the President at times as his spokesman, and if you make light of something, they then take that as an indication that the President makes light of something. You find out that your words and your inflections count a whole lot more when you get on the other end of that street. So we were very careful from that point forward. Not that we didn't have fun and enjoy ourselves, but we recognized that you have to be very careful in picking your words.

So you have one news source, which I think is important, but you also have one other thing at the White House that I think is different than the Hill: a responsibility that the President has to try to make sure his point of view gets out to the American people. Having dealt with the media and having been on the media's side of the fence, I can say that it is an adversarial relationship. The press's job is to look at a situation, take it apart, and try to interpret it for the American people, not to tell you what to think, but to try to give you at least some of the thoughts that went into it, and then hope they lead you to an appropriate decision.

I look at the same thing when you get ready to vote. I don't think the press tells you how to vote, but they are trying to influence the decisions that you will make in reaching that choice of who you are going to vote for on election day.

If you work for a president, at least give him his time at bat; let him get his words out there. Some people call it spin control; some people call it orchestrating; I call it doing the job that you were hired to do because if we don't put it out there then I don't know who does. I don't think there is anything wrong with a presidential initiative being well explained, and then allowing the press to take the information and decide how they want to portray it. I don't agree that a presidential staff should stand mute and allow someone else to step in and supplant your opinion and your initiative with their own. So whether it is spin control or whatever you call it, I do think it is important to get the presidential point of view out, to have some direction, to look not just at today, but to look two, three, sometimes four months down the road as to how you want to use today's events to influence the things you'll be doing several months later. At the White House nothing is totally separate from anything else. They just sort of build on each other. If you get yourself mired in a ditch, you don't get out of it by sitting there and spinning your wheels; you have to figure out what you can do to get going again, which is what we had to do in handling the Iran-contra situation.

This President also, I think, walked into the TV era full bore. If you think back to the images and the visual pictures that you saw as this President campaigned around the country in 1980, TV really came into its own in that presidential election. Many times the visual image was as strong or stronger than the spoken word. TV was the medium. You found other forms of journalism, particularly newspapers, changing and adapting to what TV could do, and that is to have an immediate impact on disseminating information to the American people. The *Los Angeles Times* survey a couple of years ago said that 65 percent of the people in this country get their national news from TV. For newspapers to continue to compete—I hope they do—you've got to get past just that 30-second news bite that appears every evening and hopefully past the headlines and get more of an understanding about why decisions are made. Newspapers are creating the news analysis piece which used to be on the editorial page, but now you find it on the front page; it is identified as analysis, but it is opinion. It is not a straight news story; it is somebody's opinion that does a lot more of explaining the how and why behind a situation than the traditional "who, what, where, when" that goes into a news story. That is one way I have found that newspapers tried to compete in a TV age, by bringing more off the editorial page, putting it out front and saying, "We also want to talk about why certain things happen and how they happen." That's what TV does.

The TV reports include good pictures, but it is that last ten seconds with Sam Donaldson standing on the White House lawn telling you what really happened that gets you right where it hurts. He's doing a news analysis of what the pictures mean.

What was this President able to do with TV? He was able to craft a message that would work with the television pictures. He was able to recognize that if you have a lot of American flags behind you, talk about patriotism and the things that move this country, that serves to reinforce your message. The setting does matter, because people can keep an image in their minds when you add a visual to the spoken word.

Leslie Stahl commented one time that she had done a story to talk about how the President's words really didn't fit with what he was doing, that he would stumble every now and then, and that he would sort of misstate himself. After her piece aired on CBS News she got a call from the White

House congratulating her. She was surprised and asked, "Why are you doing this? I thought it was one of the hardest pieces I've ever done." The response, "But the pictures were nice. If you tune the sound out and look at the pictures, the pictures tell the story, not the words," and that's true.

Think about the Labor Day kickoff for this [1988] presidential campaign. While I have worked for Republicans, I am not trying to stand up here and say one is better in controlling the message than the other, but here is the visual image that was projected on Labor Day. George Bush, in an open car at Disneyland with all the Americana stuff around him, versus Mike Dukakis standing in Detroit, locked arm-in-arm with labor leaders. The visuals said it all, and I think one impact this President really has had is how important it is to work with TV and how to use TV to your benefit. Television clearly became one of the primary tools he used to get his message out, and therefore to be able to lead this country.

He also looked at some of the other techniques that previous presidents had used, and I think he chose not to use some of them, such as the press conference. For this President the press conference is not the best means for him to communicate because it became more of an endurance contest than a way to get facts out about a particular decision. It reminded me of "Stump the Star," where each television correspondent wanted to get up and say, "Can I give you the one where you make the gaffe and then your staff is going to have to spend the next day or so undoing it?" rather than trying to sit there and figure out what it is that this President has been doing that people really care about and want to know more about.

I think it should be attributed to this administration's downside that they made the press conference a prime-time event by putting it on at 8:00 at night so everybody could see it. In doing that you always have to keep in mind that such a creation can also become your greatest enemy. In the case of the press conference, I don't think anybody can control what question Sam Donaldson or Chris Wallace is going to ask. But I also don't think you can control the circumstances or the expectation of the press conference, and there is a realization that this is not the best way to get the President's message out.

When I went to the White House with Senator Baker we talked about trying to make the President more accessible, not just in terms of press conferences, but in trying to find other outlets for him to get his message to the American people. We received a lot of criticism after about four or five months because there had not been a press conference since we had arrived. We sat there and were trying to deal with the question, Are you going to go ahead and do it or are you going to withstand the pressure and say no, the time is not right? We chose to withstand the pressure because the lawyers advised us that if the President were asked questions about the Iran-contra affair, all he would be able to say was, "My lawyers have told me I can't answer that." If you have a President of the United States standing up there and 75 percent of the time he says, "I can't answer that," the American people are going to think he is hiding something. One of the things we had to manage was restoring this President's ability to recapture the agenda, and you don't recapture it by going out and saying, "I can't comment" time and time again. The press conference that had been crafted into a prime-time event to some extent came back to haunt the President, because you had to acknowledge it was not the best way to get the President's message out at that point in time.

What was used to substitute for the press conference? The photo opportunity. Now I was reminded several months ago by a researcher in the White House who worked for President Nixon, that it was not President Reagan who created the "photo op," it was President Nixon. But I think President Reagan perfected the photo op, and used it, not just in office, but also in the campaigns. If you recall, Lyn Nofziger, who was the campaign press aide, would stop the President quite often on a street corner or some place, and have him answer questions. It kept him out of having to go through the day-to-day barrage—that Mike Dukakis finally realized was not to his benefit—of having the press ask you what they want to have you respond to, rather than, as a candidate or as a president, being able to lay out the things that you want to discuss.

Ronald Reagan was able to do this in the campaign of 1980 and carried it on into office. This afforded some control of the message. However, the photo op becomes somewhat of an embarrassment at times. If the president is sitting in the Oval Office with a foreign leader and the press shouts questions, there is a choice: answer them or ignore them. But the photo op became the basic tool this President used to communicate day-to-day. It is an imperfect way to do it, but as I said, it was a more manageable way for this President to get his message out.

What else is available? For President Reagan, it was the Oval Office speech, because that is purely unfiltered Reagan. There is nobody who is sitting there taking his words and translating them; there is nobody who is asking him a question. It is the President; it is the President and whatever the message is he wants to convey. I have never found a better person to look into that camera lens and have it speak his language than Ronald Reagan. I marveled as he would do videotapes. He would have a session about every two weeks. He would walk in the room cold, the words would be put on the teleprompter, and if it had to be four minutes and 58 seconds, he'd hit four minutes and 58 seconds right on the money the first time. He knew how to read something, how to time it out, pace himself so that he could fit it within a certain time period. He also knew how to make friends with the camera. The Oval Office speech for him was the television format to deliver the message and provide that forum for leadership.

There is a concern about going to the well too often, and this is what I think happened during the time that the Iran-contra episode hit, or maybe even a little bit before that.

While the President was a great communicator, you have to be very careful in using him as the *communicator*. If you are too visible, then when it is important to say something, the impact may be missed. If a major issue arises and at the appropriate time the president delivers the message, then it will have an impact. An example of this would be the way President Reagan rallied the country to support his tax cuts in 1981. But if *every* time an issue comes up the President delivers the message, it waters down his appeal over a period of time. You will not have the same kind of leadership or the same ability to lead because it becomes matter of fact. People begin to say, "Well, I wonder what he wants this time," if they say anything.

President Reagan used the Oval Office speech and the weekly radio address as his principle means to converse with the American people. When the Iran-contra episode occurred, the President appeared ill prepared in his public appearances—and then suddenly for four months you didn't hear from the President. I feel that went a long way toward creating the impression in the minds of many in this country that there must have been more to this problem than we had been told. President Reagan had been there in good times and in bad, at times when the space shuttle went down, at times when American soldiers died in the Middle East, and also at times to celebrate this country's heritage—when he stands out and looks at the Statute of Liberty. This President became a symbol for the moods of America, and his voice drove the messages that provided leadership in this country. When all of a sudden his voice was gone, it had a tremendous impact on the people of this country. That is part of what happened from November 1986 until March 1987, when the man who had been there in good times and in bad was nowhere to be seen or heard. He was still in the White House, and I believe people just hoped the President would be able to put this thing in place, tell us what really happened and make it right again. Instead, questions kept coming up and nobody was there to answer them. The impact was to leave many people still questioning whether they knew all the facts and whether the President was telling them everything that he knew. When this crisis hit, unlike previous times, the President was not there.

When you use the President as the one to deliver the message, then you do suffer the consequences when he is absent, and that's what happened in this case. But you also have to realize that an Iran-contra teaches us that you have to be able to face all of the choices—good and bad. As president, if you are a good communicator, and if you use your ability to deliver the message to lead, you have to step up into the tough political battle, as Iran-contra was, and answer, "How am I going to deal with it and how am I going to set it straight, and then how am I going to get the country and the presidency started again?"

When we went to the White House, a lot of people, particularly in the press, were saying that this presidency might be over, that the country might be waiting for the next presidential election, and that the presidency was going to be on hold for almost two years. Part of what we had to do was to dispel these notions, but also to get Ronald Reagan reestablished as the one setting the tone and the direction, and seen as a person who still had a lot that he wanted to accomplish, that his best years were not over. That meant getting him back out front, where he could use his skill as a communicator to lead the American people as he had done so often in the past.

As I said, communication—meaning the spoken word—for this President was essential. It was the way that he chose to lead this country: through the vision that he laid out, trying to present the choices to the American people, to explain fully what his goals and aspirations were for this country, and saying, "This is what America is all about. This is what people in this country care about; this is what people in this country hope to achieve in the future." Not everyone who serves in the Oval Office is going to be like this President and have this President's ability to lead by communication. That's the reason I began by looking at those who preceded him. Some who could work with TV understood the medium that was evolving during the Kennedy years. There are also presidents who ran into trouble with TV: President Nixon who supposedly won the debate with President Kennedy on radio, but lost it when people saw him perspiring on TV; or President Ford, who was captured on videotape talking about Poland not being a communist country, and he saw the replay time and time again, with no way to erase it.

That's what TV does. It has an immediate impact, and you have to understand its relationship to performing the duties and responsibilities of a president, of a governor, or of a mayor. That medium is part of what you have to work with if you are going to be able to achieve broad public goals.

If you examine the 1988 election, there has been extensive reporting about the candidates avoiding issues. I hope during the next debate that Bush and Dukakis will have more time to talk about issues rather than throwing one-liners at each other. However, they are using the techniques from the campaign trail, capturing in 20 seconds what they want to say for TV that night.

This is similar to what was done during the Iran-contra matter, trying to show that the President was not going to be totally captured by this investigation, that it was not going to drive everything that he did in the way President Nixon got caught up in Watergate. We used one phrase—"I am not a potted plant"—and repeated it three times in a speech in Wisconsin. As that speech went through the White House channels, staffers said that it's not very presidential to refer to the President as a potted plant. Others said, "It may not be presidential, but I'll guarantee you every network will carry it," and sure enough they did. That line was crafted totally for TV, designed for the President to state that he was not caught up so much in Iran-contra that he couldn't do his job. That's the role of TV now, and the candidates as they are running for the presidency have to figure out how they are going to deal with it and how they are going to incorporate it into things that they do.

Whoever is in the White House next has to also use some of the same criteria that this President used: Is TV friend or enemy? Are you a good media manipulator? Do you have a visual image, or is it better for you to find other ways to get your message out to the American people? I am not sure that either Bush or Dukakis is going to have the same ability that this President had to communicate the words and the visual images.

For each president it is important to look at the communication strengths they bring and how to incorporate those into their administration. Just as this President was very good on having a set of concise things he wanted to do, he was not as detail oriented as President Carter was. But President Reagan could talk to you about his broad vision for America, whereas President Carter could talk to you about the individual intricacies of running the government; that's a real difference. President Reagan understood his strengths and how to get those strengths out there for public consumption. So it is important to fit the person to the job—not fit the presidency to the person—and to understand all the things that impact on how you show leadership and how you communicate that leadership to a listening country.

In the Chattanooga newspaper today there is a Tom Wicker column that I found interesting. He picks up a line from Harry Truman and writes: "Truman said that the powers of the presidency amount to trying to persuade people to do the things they ought to have sense enough to do without my persuading them. That's not a job for a man paddling along in some poll taker's mainstream; that's a job for a leader, someone not afraid to hold up a standard to point the way, even on occasion to swim against the tide." That's what I think this President did. That's why I say that whether people agree or disagree with his policies, I don't think you can ever slight him for having been willing to swim against the tide. He understood what that meant and how, if you are going to have an impact and if you are going to be a leader, you need some ability, if not to control completely, at least to have a hand on the lever that provides direction, either right or left, for the country.

QUESTION: I think that most people are fully aware of the significance of rhetoric and communication skills for the president to get his message across. This is something that is very clear. To what extent can rhetoric and communication aides help the president improve his rhetoric and communication skills? It seems to me there is an inherent talent involved, that if you are very skillful like President Reagan you could do it perfectly fine. Mr. Carter loved to talk about the many details, and he did that during his administration and last year when he came here. It seems to me that communication skills are something inherent. How could you help the President in office to develop those skills, and if he can, how much time and energy do the postwar American presidents allocate to the polishing of their rhetorical skills?

MR. GRISCOM: I think that if a staff functions properly, they complement the strengths that a president brings to office. If President Carter was detail oriented, then you have to make sure that you support the way that he wants to communicate. I think the worst thing politicians can do is to come in and become something that they are not, because when you do that it raises the question of whether you are hiding something or trying to overlook something that may be very much part of your character and part of the process that you go through to make decisions. So the first thing I say is, you adapt yourself to that person and to his style.

In the case of President Reagan, you are right. I think his years of training got him to the point where he could stand up and deliver a speech. The written word was only about 10 percent of what he could do once he got up in front of a mike to deliver it. He had a very strong delivery.

But let me tell you what somebody in the position I had can do. You can go to Moscow and sit down and talk to Soviet citizens, talk to our people who are stationed in the Soviet Union about their goals and aspirations, what they think of this country. You then match that up with what this President has been trying to do for the past eight years in talking tough at times, but also in trying to say that the strength that we showed early has brought us to the point where we could sign the first actual reductions in nuclear arms. You pull all those pieces together and you recognize that you've got a president who can probably stand in front of a group of students at Moscow State University whom he has never seen and disarm them by being willing to take questions, something that their own leaders have never done in their own country.

As a staff you attempt to complement the strengths of the president. In the case of Moscow State University, we recognized that the Soviet Union was in a time of change—and they continue to change. Change is very difficult in that country. They are concerned that by changing they are going to lose traditions, things that have been important to them over the years. We have a president who can talk about the fact that America is a country of change, that people from around the world come here and locate in this country, and they have a chance to do things that they wanted to do in their own country but couldn't, for whatever reason. You find students in that audience saying that they did not realize that America was a country made up of immigrants, that they had no idea of that. But you also have a chance for this President, because of his ability to communicate, to talk about this country and what this country is all about, to do what we call a little civics lesson inside that speech. We were able to give the students a better feel for what Americans really do believe and what their hopes are, that we are not sitting over here waiting to push a button to blow them up and that we hope they are not sitting there waiting to push a button to blow us up. We had a chance to explain a little bit more about what this country is founded on, and to reinforce that, to leave a copy of the works of Jefferson and Washington and Lincoln in the Moscow State University Library.

If a staff works properly it takes the strengths of the President, but also the weaknesses, and builds around those. You don't try to go in and recreate something that's not there, because if you do that it will not come across as genuine; it will come across as very hollow in the process. Because this President had core convictions and some basic principles that he stood on, along with that ability to be able to stand up and speak, you had the foundations to build from, and that's what we were able to do.

QUESTION: To what extent do the postwar American presidents spend time and energy polishing their rhetoric and communication skills?

MR. GRISCOM: Let's go much past postwar. I think TV really changed things in this country because that became, as I said, communication; information could be disseminated immediately. Almost as soon as it was said, you could have your TV set on and be watching and listening to someone telling you what this person said and why it's important. So you had to recognize that you have a new set of journalists who are on-the-spot commentators. How can you then deal with them? In this country where public opinion is very important—and that's why I used the Vietnam War analogy early on—if you don't have the public support, you are swimming upstream and you are not going to get there. In a country where pollsters poll almost at the drop of a hat, you've got to make sure that you have a chance at least to help shape the agenda, to get your point of view across, and that as that message is being delivered into homes around this country, and around the world now, that at least there is an opportunity for you to help shape and form what that message is. If you don't use those opportunities, then you've got a void; and believe me, the void will be filled.

When I was communication director for the White House, I had a group that met each morning to look at the messages for that day and to refine them if necessary. I also had a planning group that drew from all the major areas within the White House; our group looked sometimes as much as four months down the road. We started planning for the Moscow summit the week after the Washington summit ended, thinking then not only about what it was that we might do when we went to Moscow, but also what the events would be leading up to that. If we were going to talk about individual freedoms in Moscow, shouldn't we at least be setting that scenario and laying out some of those themes in advance? The answer is yes, we should. If all of a sudden we went to Moscow and started talking about something foreign that nobody had heard before, then that would have an impact too. People will say, "Why did the President do that?" It is a building process. If we knew that we had a tough issue coming in Congress like contra aid, then we needed to try and get the President's message out there to help shape the debate, even recognizing that we might not be successful. But we had got to try to at least show both sides of the argument.

One of the things that I'm trying to do at the University of Tennessee at Chattanooga is not to come in and push one political point of view over the other, but to bring in all sides and let people listen to the arguments and then decide who is right and who is wrong. I think that's part of what planning at the White House and communication strategy at the White House is all about. You've got to be willing to stand up if you believe in it and put your point of view out there for people to hear it, then let them decide if you are right or wrong. I think that's the option that you have to work with, and I think you will find it becomes even more critical in succeeding administrations.

QUESTION: What was the cause of the communications breakdown within the administration during Iran-contra?

MR. GRISCOM: I have tried not to criticize those who preceded us in the White House. Don Regan gave us a piece of advice that first Saturday when we went to the White House. He said, "Get a flak jacket and put it on backwards." I think people expect that a chief of staff is just that, that he knows everything that is going on, and I think he ought to. Something that Ken may want to examine at some point through the Miller Center is the staff function for a president. Most people think of a chief of staff as the person who sits right by the president, who knows all the levers being pulled, and who can stop them before something happens. That is not the way it works. You have a chief of staff, but you also have a national security adviser, and they have almost equal access to the president. The chief of staff knows what the national security adviser is sending in, but the national security adviser also sends in each day a brown folder that has the president's security briefing in it. Sometimes included in that briefing in the fold-over flap are a couple of little things that he might want to look at, but they are decision memos. Quite often a chief of staff doesn't even know those have gone in.

I think the next president really needs to sit down and look very seriously at the staffing of the White House and the responsibilities that key White House staff should assume. This President gets faulted for the fact that he delegated a lot away. I'm not sure that that's so wrong, because I think you can have the other side of it where you get so mired down in details that you lose the vision of what you ought to be doing. I think a president ought to have a vision and direction to lead this country; he ought to have a handful of things he really cares about, but that also requires you to have staff that understands their role. It is what I call the Howard Baker rule: no surprises.

In putting the summit together, I saw the President three times so he would know what I was doing, the ideas I was coming up with, to make sure that he did not get surprised in Moscow. I wanted to make sure he knew what was happening, because I think that's the role of a good staff, to make sure that you support the principal and that you don't surprise him.

What happened in Iran-contra? I think several things went awry. One, I don't think there ever was a clear policy as to what we were ultimately trying to achieve in Central America. I will be very frank with you. I was serving on the Hill when the policy was first enunciated. There were those within the administration who felt that our role was to overthrow the Sandinistas. There were those who felt our role was to support the contras and bring pressure to change the government. There were those who felt that we should be out there in some role to prevent the Soviets from establishing a beachhead in Central America. But I don't think any one person ever really sat down and said, "Here is what we are going to do," and then drove the policy to make it happen. Therefore, what you ran into was a situation where you had what is best called a leadership gap. Certain people within the National Security Council (NSC), I am convinced, stepped in and filled that void, and they started trying to drive the policy for what they thought the goal was, which was to make sure that there was a democratic government in Nicaragua. You know the result.

Where did the communication breakdown occur? I would like to know, because we walked into a White House that was caught up in all this, and we were trying to sort out very quickly what went wrong. If George Shultz and Cap Weinberger were saying this was bad policy, why weren't people listening? If the NSC had an operational unit set up, why didn't somebody know it? I have seen the NSC operation and I know what goes through it; for me it is hard to understand why somebody in an oversight role did not catch this, but they didn't. The bottom line is, knowing that it went this way, why did somebody not give the President the information he needed to prevent himself from going out there and publicly adding to the sense of confusion that happened in November of 1986? Those are answers that I don't have.

I think your question is very good, but also I think what it argues for is to make sure that when a new administration comes in, they should learn from the mistakes of this administration. You ought to learn and profit from your mistakes.

One of the real errors I saw was assuming that a chief of staff is totally responsible for everything that happens to the President without him having the authority to handle that role. If I had been Don Regan, I would have stood up early on and said, "Wait a minute. If I am going to take all the slings and arrows, then I want to have the ability to control them." And he did not have that. That's an internal argument that goes back to the Kissinger days: What is the role of the national security adviser, and how does he interact with the chief of staff and the President of the United States? The national security adviser wants to make sure he has direct access to the president. I'm not saying he shouldn't, but I think if the chief of staff is going to bear the responsibility he should be able to say wait a minute, or to at least make sure that there is a funnel coming in so that he knows what is happening. Otherwise you can run into the same problem all over again.

It gets down to the type of people that you bring in, and whether they understand the responsibility of the role that they have. To my way of thinking this role is to support the President of the United States to the best of your ability, and if you see something going wrong that you don't agree with, bring it to the president's attention. That is all you can do. If the president then decides to go forward, he is the president, the commander in chief, and he has that right. He was elected by the people to do it. If you don't bring it to his attention, then I think that you have not fulfilled your job as a staff person, because supporting him is part of what your role is. I don't care who it is in that office; there are so many details and so much is going on so fast that no president can know everything to the nth degree all the time. That's why you've got to have good people to support you. Hopefully, that's one of the lessons that comes out.

QUESTION: You seem to be arguing that the function of a press conference is for the president to get his message out; and yet he can get his message out with one of the Oval Office speeches. To me the whole notion of a press conference is give-and-take, a responsibility that the president has to the people as a whole to respond to questions that the press gives. How would you respond to the idea that there's a responsibility involved?

MR. GRISCOM: I don't disagree with your point. Let me go back and explain a little bit more about the press conference. One of the first things that Dan Rather said about this President when we went to the White House was the test of whether he could still govern was going to be whether he could take the questions of the White House press corps. I thought that was going way too far. I think there has to be some common ground between the president and the press, particularly the White House press, so that you come to some common terms as to what their role is in getting the news and information out to the American people. In addition there must be consideration of the president's responsibility in making sure that he does not get so caught up and has to stand up and say time and time again, "I can't answer that." I feel that becomes a perception problem for the president and will make people think that he is hiding something. I don't advocate doing away with the press conference; I don't think that you should. I think a press conference is an appropriate training ground and keeps you current, active, and agile with what is going on and what people are concerned with.

When Senator Baker opened the Senate each day, he had five to ten minutes on the floor in front of the chamber with the press that would come in and talk about what was going on that day. I think that is something maybe the next president should think about doing. Each morning the president could start the day by bringing in 10 or 15 reporters, alternating around, to sit in the Oval Office and say, "I want to give you something that I'm going to be doing today," and then sit there and listen to them and answer their questions.

What I am saying about press conferences are two things: one, to get off the idea that it is a prime-time event. I think that's a mistake this administration made, because a press conference at two o'clock in the afternoon is just as good as one at eight o'clock at night. You focus more on audience share than quality of questions in prime time. The other thing is to take the press conference outside of the White House. What is wrong with coming to Charlottesville and doing a press conference right here or going to Chicago or wherever? Who ever said that the only ones to ask the president a question are those people who cover the White House on a day-to-day basis? During the time we were there, we did two press conferences outside the White House, and they were the best press conferences I saw because what you got then were questions about what is really on the minds of people in this country, not about what it is that you have to say to get yourself on the news that night. I don't think that every press conference should require that the television networks ask questions.

If you look at the past eight years, there are about 80 percent of the press corps who have covered this President from the very beginning who have never had a chance at a press conference to ask him a question. Why is it that TV correspondents have the best questions? I don't think they do. What I am trying to figure out is how do you get away from that notion? How do you change it from a television spectacle event into an event that provides information to the public and answers their questions? Maybe what you do is from time to time have people calling in to the President. But what I want to see is more back and forth that really gets questions on the minds of certain reporters in this country, not necessarily what is on the minds of the people who cover the White House day to day and what may be able to get them on the news that night. That's the point I was trying to make.

QUESTION: When President Ford followed Nixon, there was a sense of decency and a fresh air blowing through the White House. There was a feeling that when Senator Baker followed Donald Regan, there would be a sense of greater credibility, an impression of clean air coming through. It didn't seem to happen. Were Senator Baker's hands tied too tightly?

MR. GRISCOM: I agree with you. I think the conventional wisdom in Washington was: We are going to get rid of the bad guys and bring in "one of our own," because here is Senator Baker who had been serving for 18 years, and all of a sudden everything is just going to change. What people tend to lose sight of is that we were brought in to deal with a tough political problem for this President, to try to get his agenda back on track. To do that meant that there were some tough decisions that were going to have to be made, that we weren't just all of a sudden going to be able to say, "Well, we are just going to forget all this," or "whatever you ask for we are going to give you."

There was a lot of criticism about the veto of the highway bill, if you recall; that happened within the first two weeks we were there. Everybody said, "Senator Baker knows Congress; why did he let that happen? There is no way you are going to win." What people lost sight of is that there was still a President who was sitting in the Oval Office who was President. Our job was to give him the best advice we could, to work with him. But that's Senator Baker's strength as well, that he wasn't going to try to replace the President with his own thinking, but to try to give him his best advice, and once a decision is made to carry it out. I think that while we might have done something different on the highway bill, the

President made a choice; he fought a good fight and lost by one vote. It showed that he was still ready to fight. He went up to the Senate, spoke to the Republican senators trying to get that last vote, and you even had Senator Kennedy after it was over commending the President for the conviction he had to stand by what he believed.

What I think happened within some quarters in Washington is they forgot that it wasn't as if when we came in everything that had gone before would just be removed. The only thing that got removed was when Don Regan and some of his key staff left; we came in with Senator Baker and two or three of us. The playing field was exactly the same; what we were trying to do was level it again, but in doing so you have to deal with the circumstances that existed. If we could have started all over, I can guarantee you we would have gotten a big eraser and said, "Iran-contra is gone, let's get rid of it." Some of the toughest work I've ever done is having to sit there day in and day out and figure out what to do today to make sure that you (1) keep the story out of the White House as best you can; (2) protect the President's interests and make sure his point of view is getting across; and (3) show that he still has other things he wants to do, that he can still drive an agenda and is still going to be part of the Washington structure that is going to make things happen and is going to set policy in this country.

Part of our mistake—if I can term it that—is that we allowed a perception to be created that all of a sudden things were going to be so much different just by Senator Baker coming in and some of us coming in with him. After the fact we said that we should have probably done more to hold down that expectation level, because coming in we knew the problems we had and what we were going to have to deal with. In doing so we were not going to be the ultimate decisionmakers, the President of the United States was. We had to follow his direction after we gave him our advice. It's very different when somebody else is at the top making the final choice than when you are a United States senator and you make it yourself.

QUESTION: A lot of people were surprised when Senator Baker dropped out of the presidential primary race and took the chief of staff job. Could you give us your insight as to why he did that?

MR. GRISCOM: I think Senator Baker feels very strongly that when a president asks you to do something you have to do it. When this President called him and asked him to become chief of staff, how could he tell the President no? There is a sense of duty and responsibility that he feels any American ought to feel when the President asks you to make some kind of sacrifice—in this case it was to give up his own thought about running—that you ought to do it if you can come and help him, and that's really what it got down to. In the final analysis he said, "How would I set aside what the President asked me to do to help him, in return for something that I might want to do but might not be successful in achieving?" And so he decided that the answer was if the President asks you, you have to say yes. I think if he asked him again today to come back, he would drop what he is doing and go back one more time.

QUESTION: Scholars of the presidency have called attention to the emergence of this form of communication where presidents often go over the heads of Congress and appeal directly to the people and have them bring pressure to bear on the legislature. You alluded in passing to the contra aid fight. Part of the downside which scholars have pointed to is that no matter what amount of capital a president may have, how many congressmen will back that up? I wonder whether contra aid would be a good instance of this. To the extent that you were involved in mapping out the speeches in which the President did appeal directly to the public in that fashion, were you concerned about conserving some of that capital for future use? What kinds of attempts were made to ensure that he would not exhaust his reserves?

MR. GRISCOM: If you remember, I made the point that I think the President's message got so diluted because they went to the well so often and kept using him as the only means to communicate. If you have an attorney general or a secretary of state or a secretary of the treasury, all of whom are capable, why not let them get out, carry some of the water, and then bring the President in at the moment when you really need to have an impact?

In the case of Iran-contra, we were going against public opinion, because the policy was never fully worked out. At that point the White House staff said, "But there is nobody else with any credibility left who could talk about it other than the President, so you have to put him out there." We really questioned a lot whether to go forward with that last appeal. If you remember, the networks all refused to carry it. They said, "It isn't newsworthy," and that also troubled me. I asked, "At what point do television people all of a sudden become not only the people who cover the news but also the ones who are going to determine whether something is newsworthy or not." And they said, "If the President will add this to his speech then we'll cover it." I thought that really was stepping way over the boundary that exists between the media and an officeholder, in this case the President.

What we were looking at is an eight-year presidency. You have to go back and say, "Well, if we hadn't done this a couple of years ago then maybe we could have come back in with this reservoir and done it." But you also had certain people who were trained to say, "Now the only one who can deliver the message is the President." Many of those were some of the conservative followers of this President who said, "If you don't use him then you are not using all the abilities that you have to try to move public opinion, and therefore, we are going to be critical of you and are going to let it be known

that the White House held back from using the President."
So you've also got those pressures.

We ran into that quite often with the nominations to the
Supreme Court of Bork, Ginsburg, and Kennedy. I know this
one well because I sat in the Roosevelt Room and had to tell
Judge Bork that the President was not going to do a televised
speech right before the committee vote on his nomination.
There was no doubt what was going to happen: They were
going to give him an unfavorable vote. If you shoot your best
shot then, you can't pull it back out when it gets to the full
Senate. The President goes out, uses everything he has, and
the committee still votes him down. But there are a lot of
people who have a hard time understanding that you hold
back a little bit for impact many times, and if the one thing
that you have that has the greatest impact is the President
himself, you don't throw him out there just helter-skelter.

Maybe one should sit down on the front end and figure
out whether you are going to be a four-year president or plan
to serve eight years, and then really map out what you do as
a president to try to move the agenda. You should decide
when to make sure that somebody else is carrying the
message for you so that you don't use up all your capital, and
when it gets down to it the TV networks won't say, "Well,
look, this isn't newsworthy because we've heard him talk
about it time and time again." That's what you ran into with
the contra aid battle in the final analysis.

QUESTION: I understand that you wrote the speech at
Moscow State University which was originally to be broadcast
across the Soviet Union, but was not. Was the speech
previewed by Soviet officials? What difference would that
have made in preparation for that speech if you knew there
was just going to be your college audience versus the whole
nation?

MR. GRISCOM: It was not reviewed in advance at all. We
had hoped that they would broadcast it, but they made the

comment back to us that they had technical problems as to why they could not make that happen. I'll let you take that for what it's worth. We were disappointed because we wanted a chance for this President to be talking, as you know, to the whole of the Soviet Union. Whether they rebroadcast it or not—they told us they were going to do that—I have yet to find out.

I guess in the final analysis that having allowed 600, 700, or 800 college students in the Soviet Union to hear the President, there is no way that you can come behind the President of the United States and say, "Don't believe him." They have to wrestle with that themselves. I said that it would have been much better to get it all over the country, but that audience right there maybe was the best setting because these are young people; these are the next leaders in that country, and they are going to have to be sitting there raising the questions with the current leaders about why they have been taught one thing, and this President of the United States who has been allowed to come in here has told us something different. They are going to have to wrestle with that and reconcile the differences that exist. We'll have to see what the impact is.

I know the speech was reprinted and was passed out in some of the other cities in the Soviet Union by some of our embassy people, but clearly the ability to have had it broadcast live would have been preferable. If he gets rebroadcast then the same thing can happen that happened with Tom Brokaw's interview with Gorbachev where they edited Gorbachev's answers, and you may not get the full extent of what the President said in the total context in which he said it.

You learn from each time, and we learned that you've got to push a little bit harder next time around. When we initially raised the idea of doing the Moscow State University speech, after we said what we wanted to do about letting the President make some prepared remarks and then take Q and A, there was silence. Then the person with whom I was negotiating said, "What is Q and A?" I answered, "That's where the President is going to get questions from the audience and is going to respond to them." And then they huddled for a minute and came back and said, "Who is going to write the questions? Is he going to write them himself and answer them?" We said, "No, no, no. You all will do it." So then they went back and came back in and said, "We write the questions and then give them to him?" I said, "You all do whatever you want to. All we are asking is this: After he makes the speech we want the President to be able to have students—not 40-, 50-, or 60-year-old men standing up—to stand up and ask a question from the audience, and the President will respond to it. They said, "You mean he will answer it right there?" I said, "Sure." This was something very foreign to them. They had no idea; they had never seen this happen. I found it interesting that after the President did this, that during the same summit week General Secretary Gorbachev held the first press conference in the Soviet Union that has ever been held by a general secretary.

Again, it is small things like that that may be opening it up a little bit and creating a somewhat freer exchange of ideas in the Soviet Union. If it is only an incremental movement, at least there is some impact, I think.

QUESTION: It seems that Reagan's policies are increasingly generating a political process by trying to turn political events into entertainment, by broadcasting press conferences during prime time. They seem to be concentrating more on image than on substance. Is there any solution to this, or is it just going to get worse and worse?

MR. GRISCOM: Unfortunately you find those in office and those who are campaigning for office having to fit into that environment because that's the way the majority of news is delivered to the American people, in those 20- or 30-second sound bites. You are going to have to change a couple of things. One, you are going to have to get people, and particularly young people, back to where they really want to sit down and read past the headlines, so that they want to pick up a newspaper and find a little bit more about what is going on, and not just think that because something is on TV and they catch a glimpse of it that that's enough. We were talking at the University of Tennessee a couple of weeks ago about a certain event that had been discussed on "Nightline," and the students sat there and said almost verbatim what had been said on "Nightline." And I said, "Fine, now tell me what it meant," and there was no response. What troubles me is that we are not stimulating people to think past the headlines, to think past the sound bite, to get them to want to ask questions and find out more own their own. I think the first thing we need to do is figure out how we reeducate ourselves so that we want to go back and read past what we are being told.

The second thing is that hopefully we will have more presidential debates rather than fewer, and maybe we can get away from always having journalists as questioners. I think they ought to be there sometimes, but I'd like to see the two candidates really have a debate and actually quiz each other. It may be a knock-down-and-drag-out, but what's wrong with that? What's wrong with them sitting out there and probing each other and asking each other questions? Asking, "Why did you say this?" Maybe you would get more than Joe Isuzu answers and a Boston Harbor one-liner. Why didn't somebody the other night talk about what we are going to do about our trade situation? Why don't we press each other and say, "What are you going to do about the deficit in this country? How are you really going to deal with it? And are you definitely going to put social security or anything like that off-limits?" Those questions are going to have to be wrestled with, but we are not getting that. Part of it, I think, is that just as it is sometimes said that "we the people" means we get the type of government we deserve, I think we get the type of coverage we deserve.

When the media really went after Quayle, the people said, "Wait a minute, you went too far"; all of a sudden you saw the media backing up. Why don't we do that more often and say, "We want to know more and we want to hear more; we want to see more than just a nice visual image. We want to know what is going on." Why not call on television particularly then to provide that opportunity in that forum, to give you more of a public affairs type approach than just trying to encapsulate things? I think that what it takes is for people to stand up and say, "We want better than what we are getting right now," because otherwise you are going to end up with the same type of campaign that you have right now, and that is trying to figure out where I can get the best picture so that when you see it on the air you are looking at *where* somebody was, not necessarily *what* it was that they said.

CHAPTER 6

In the Market
for a Little Greatness[*]

RUSSELL BAKER

After Governor Dukakis's great speech, George Bush absolutely had to make a great speech too. Everybody said so, at least everybody who could get access to a television camera, and after you heard those TV-savvy guys and women announce that George Bush would have to make the greatest speech he had ever made in his life, how could you have the cheek to disagree with them?

Because they knew, didn't they? That's why they were on television. Because they knew. Knew when you had to make the greatest speech of your life. Knew when you could get by with a lesser speech, with maybe the fourth- or fifth-best speech of your life.

Knew when you had to make a terrible speech because making a great one would be catastrophic.

Slice-of-life vignette:

---

[*]*Reprinted from the* New York Times, *24 August 1988,* A25.

"Do you agree with everybody else, Jason, that it's absolutely essential this week for George Bush to make the worst speech he's ever made in his life?"

"You are reading my mind, Stepmore. As I said in the 1952 campaign after Adlai Stevenson made his third great speech in three days, unless Stevenson comes down from the oratorical heights and starts making speeches as bad as Eisenhower he's doomed. And do you know why I said that, Stepmore?"

"I do indeed, Jason. You enunciated the famous political principle that when you're running against a hero beloved by all humanity, everybody will get mad at you if you make speeches that make the hero's seem tenth-rate."

Enough vignette. Back to the Dukakis-Bush Greatest Speech of His Life competition:

Yes, Bush met the test. Sure, you slept through it, but everybody with access to a TV camera loaded up on caffeine, and afterward they all said it was the greatest speech of Bush's life.

Not one of the great speeches of all time. Not Demosthenes, Cicero, or Patrick Henry. Not Abraham Lincoln at Gettysburg, much less Ronald Reagan at the Teleprompter. But for Bush, great. Greatest speech he ever made.

Just like Dukakis's great speech, not an all-time great speech, but still the greatest Dukakis ever made. Each man did what he had to do. Such performance spells "great candidate."

When the going gets tough, these are candidates who can deliver great speeches. Don't think that isn't bad news for America's enemies, especially liberals, whose failure to produce a single speech maker capable of making the greatest speech of his life under pressure gives ample proof of how far this nasty gang has drifted from—

Can somebody toss me the cliché I'm looking for?

—from the mainstream, of course—how far this evil crowd has drifted from the mainstream.

Why are these men, Dukakis and Bush, able to make the greatest speeches of their lives when the caffeine-packed people who enjoy access to television say they've got to do it?

Because they have great speech writers. Don't be coyly cynical, don't pretend you thought all along that the greatest speeches of their lives, which these two splendid candidates made when they had to, were written by the men who made them. Nobody is as unwised-up as that anymore.

Greatest speeches of men's lives are written by professionals, by people who not only hold Ph.D.'s from Speechwriting A. & M., but have spent years at the famous tax-deductible Loquacious Foundation mastering the art of writing the greatest speeches of people's lives.

During World War II Winston Churchill, speaking in his own words, said, "Give us the tools, and we will finish the job." Nowadays great men say, "Give me the greatest speech of my life and I will read it in a way that will knock the socks off the caffeine-soaked television speech appraisers."

There are people, mean-spirited people, who sneer at our democratic institutions, saying, "If the speech is such a vital index to greatness, we ought to vote for the speech writers instead of the people who read their words aloud to the wakeful hundreds of the caffeine-besotted."

Nonsense? Of course. Greatness consists not in what a speech says, but in the performance its buyer gives while reading it off the Teleprompter. Is his cheek rouge effective? Is his eye contact with the camera fetching?

And, of course, the central question: Does the candidate have the greatness to choose the one speech writer who can write him the best speech of his life? Bush and Dukakis did. A lesser man might have erred, chosen a plagiarist, and opened the greatest speech of his life by thundering, "How long, O Catiline, will you continue to abuse our patience?"

III.

THE RHETORIC
OF FOREIGN POLICY

CHAPTER 7

The Marshall Plan
and the Harvard Speech

FORREST C. POGUE

NARRATOR: The debate over who is the greatest American in the 20th century will continue for years to come. Franklin Roosevelt has adherents; Dwight Eisenhower has others. But if the group which worked intimately with George Marshall were to be polled, a large number of them would choose General Marshall.

We are fortunate to have with us Forrest Pogue, the author and editor of a multivolume biography of Marshall and a collection of some of his definitive writings. To mention a few of his texts, they include: *The Supreme Command* (1954); a three volume study, *George C. Marshall: Education of a General, 1889-1939* (1963); *Ordeal and Hope, 1939-42* (1966); and *Organizer of Victory, 1943-45* (1973). He also coauthored or contributed to: *The Meaning of Yalta* (1956); *Command Decisions* (1960); *Total War and Cold War* (1962); and *D-Day: The Normandy Invasion in Retrospect* (1970). In terms of quantity, and more importantly quality, Forrest Pogue has earned a place in the forefront of those researching and writing on General Marshall.

Those who knew men like Lovett, Acheson, McCloy, and others who surrounded Marshall recall the many stories and vignettes that they offered about General Marshall. He is supposed to be the author of the famous saying that "in decision making, don't fight the problem," of the requirement that staff produce a one-page summary on the top of memoranda "telling me what you want me to do," of a viewpoint that stressed the responsibilities of public service, and many others. A lifetime of research devoted to General Marshall is a worthy enterprise. Forrest Pogue was director of the research program at the George Marshall Library. During World War II he was one of eight historians who were recruited to chronicle the history of the conflict in the European theater. Indeed he was one of three of that group of eight who actually took part in the Omaha Beach landing, although the three stayed on the LSTs so that somebody would survive to tell the story. From that time on, he has continued to clarify and preserve important truths about this great man, General Marshall, who was respected most by those who knew him best.

Forrest Pogue will tell us about the speech announcing the Marshall Plan, but there may be other issues and he will be pleased to answer any questions.

MR. POGUE: The reason I've decided to talk about Marshall's contribution to the speech is because lately a number of provocative remarks and statements have been made. I remember being shocked some years ago when I was one of the questioners of members of a panel who had worked with Truman and Marshall. Averell Harriman dominated the conversation and said: "Of course, General Marshall had nothing to do with the Marshall Plan." He was challenged immediately by Phillip Jessup, Paul Porter, and three or four others. So Harriman responded, "Oh, yes, he did make the speech." The trouble is that this sort of thing has a way of getting into books. A number of you have read the most interesting book, *The Wise Men*, in which one of the writers says categorically that Acheson probably had more to do with the speech than Marshall did. Acheson did have his part in the speech and has written about his role, but I say Mr. Acheson was not being entirely fair to a man named George Kennan.

General Marshall insisted over and over that he did not write the Marshall Plan speech, just as Mr. Acheson told me that *he* did not write the Marshall Plan speech. But General Marshall did not say that he had nothing to do with that speech. What I will try to show is that the actions which Marshall took—the things that he said as far back as the fall of 1945—made it possible later for him to talk about the United States adopting the Marshall Plan. In his final report to the secretary of war, in the late summer of 1945, Marshall wrote a statement on postwar policy that pointed toward the Marshall Plan and the Marshall Plan speech. He didn't actually write that report either; it was written by a man named Jim Shepley, whom Marshall had brought into the army as a captain because he liked his articles in *Time-Life*. Marshall borrowed Shepley from Henry Luce, first to write the report, which was based on tons of material furnished by Marshall's personal staff, and then to go with him to China during the first phase of that mission.

This report contained Marshall's beliefs that had guided his actions since 1939. Since the end of World War I, Marshall had rejected isolationism. Therefore, in this final report he wanted to make clear that the United States could not revert to isolationism; that it was essential for the United States, which had become one of the great powers of the world, and one of the wealthiest powers, to continue to be strong in peacetime. Marshall believed that it was impossible for the United States to duck the responsibility of world leadership.

General Marshall made a statement expressing this opinion on the day he left the military on 26 November 1945. In the Pentagon's great courtyard, amidst representatives from the Army, Navy, and Air Force, he said in effect: "The war is won, you've won it, but the peace is still to be won and you have to win that because most of the countries of the world find themselves exhausted economically, financially, and physically. If the world is to get on its feet, if the productive facilities of the world are to be restored, if democratic processes in many countries are to resume their functioning, a strong lead and definite assistance from the United States will be necessary."

It is easy to dismiss this statement as mere "rhetoric." But Marshall was not given to "rhetoric"; he usually crossed it out when someone wrote it into a speech. Later I can find almost these exact words in the Marshall Plan speech. This statement, among others, indicates that Marshall was reaching toward something akin to the Marshall Plan long before the Marshall Plan speech was written. Others reached the same conclusion but in a different way. But this idea did not come to Marshall as something that was laid on his desk by George Kennan, Will Clayton, or Dean Acheson; it certainly did not come out of Acheson's Delta Council speech. These were things that Marshall was thinking about a great deal but which he never imagined he'd have anything to do with. He assumed on that day, 26 November 1945, that his work was over. He was past the Army's age of retirement, and he was tired. He had been chief of staff for over six years and been fighting a war globally, and helping to sustain people globally.

The business of feeding part of Europe was not a new concept because we had been feeding, as well as arming, part of Europe for some time. Marshall was one of the few people in the world who had been dealing with this responsibility on an international scale. To indicate that all of this initiative came from a few people at the working level in the bowels of the State Department is a little unfair.

Let's look at Marshall from the time he became secretary of state. The first job he had to perform in his new position was to represent the United States at the Moscow meeting of the foreign ministers. He set out to learn the issues that would be set forth in arguments with Molotov or presumably with Bevin or Bidault. It is interesting to note, in view of the fact that Mr. Truman later said Secretary of State James F. Byrnes coddled the Russians and that therefore he had to have someone new, that the men who briefed Marshall were, for the most part, Byrnes' staff. They were telling Marshall the same things that they had been telling Byrnes. For example, on the day that Marshall became secretary of state, Ambassador Walter Bedell Smith sent him a memo concerning the problems of dealing with the Russians. Smith made a most interesting statement that "if it were necessary to divide Europe in order not to allow the Russians to have their way, then let it be done." That statement was written for Byrnes, but it was part of the briefing that Marshall went through when he became secretary of state.

On the afternoon of 21 February 1947, Marshall was at Princeton University to receive an honorary degree and make an important speech. That speech was not carefully constructed. Marshall wrote the bulk of it himself and later termed it "hashed together." However, one thing that we know was written by someone else is the most quoted part of the speech: that one couldn't understand modern problems unless one understood the Peloponnesian Wars.

I occasionally get letters from classics scholars who ask how well Marshall read Greek. I respond, probably as well as he read Latin, which he never studied. He liked the statement, though; I'm sure he had read part of Thucydides. The concepts were certainly familiar to him. But he actually put together the bulk of this speech by going back to some of the ideas contained in that November 1945 Pentagon speech: "we cannot be isolationists any more"; "we cannot depend on the oceans to protect us"; "we cannot wait for two years for our friends to protect us while we re-arm"; and "we owe something to the world which looks to us for leadership." Some of these ideas he mentioned again when accepting the 1953 Nobel Peace Prize in Oslo.

Anyway, we know that he was getting his own ideas across at this point, though he did not write any part of the

Truman Doctrine speech. While he was on his way to Princeton, a telephone call came to the State Department from the British ambassador. Acheson took it and the ambassador said, "I have a memo from Ernest Bevin. He wants it delivered to General Marshall personally." Acheson said, "I'm filling in for Marshall while he is away. I'm going to have to help make suggestions for a reply, so why don't you let me have the memo over the weekend so I can have something to report to Marshall on Monday." And you know the contents of the memo. Bevin reported that Britain was running out of money and that it could not continue with its commitments to Greece and Turkey after the first of April. Bevin was recommending that the United States assume that burden. Acheson and other staff members worked all that weekend on suggestions for a policy. When Marshall got back on Monday, before he received the official text of Bevin's cable, he had already discussed and approved the general direction of the suggestions.

It is an interesting thing that George Kennan was involved in preparing the Truman Doctrine speech. His influence preceded his work on the policy planning staff, which began on the first of May. Kennan was borrowed from assignment at the National War College by Acheson to help prepare recommendations to the President that led to the Truman Doctrine speech. Of course Kennan got into trouble with the White House because he felt that the rhetoric of the Truman Doctrine speech (which he did not help draft) was too strong, just as Marshall and Charles Bohlen thought it was when they saw it later. Though all three strongly advocated the containment of Russia—Kennan above all—they felt that foreign policy shouldn't be built on rhetoric. Marshall said more than once: "You don't slap a man in the face when you've got only one-and-a-half divisions ready to go. You take a firm stand but you also leave yourself room to maneuver."

At any rate, Marshall and Acheson recommended to the President that we assume these burdens. In large part because of the White House, a broad statement was added, that any country that wanted to stand up to forces inside and forces outside could look to us. As far as Marshall was concerned, this statement had one effect: it led to the appointment of an ad hoc committee to start studying priorities and resources. But it is quite important to keep in mind the fact that the Marshall Plan did not come directly from the Truman speech.

The Truman Doctrine forced an examination of priorities. If every nation wanting help suddenly asked for it, what was the United States to do? Eisenhower (with Secretary Patterson and members of the Budget Bureau) probably sparked Acheson's reaction by asking in effect, "Just how many commitments must we take on this week, next week, in two weeks? We need a study of this." An ad hoc committee, picked by the State-War-Navy Coordinating Committee, began that study and by April had information on overall American commitments. When I tell you that Korea was the number one priority, you'll better understand that this was not a plan for what we call the Marshall Plan. In the process of working up information for the use of Marshall and the State Department—a number of studies were going on, not only in the State Department but also in the Treasury and Commerce Departments—you have the genesis of the Marshall Plan speech. The important point is how these strands took shape as the Marshall Plan speech.

Some of this material appears in the Acheson Delta Council speech, some of which Joseph Jones wrote. Jones says that before writing part of that speech he talked with Walter Lippmann, who had written some articles along these lines. Ronald Steel suggests that the whole Marshall concept was really Lippmann's. The great trouble with that line of thought is that Lippmann's writings at various times consider everything, including the Fourteen Points. A writer who is so prolific suggests any number of things. However, what is always forgotten in debates of who wrote what is who actually focused the thoughts into a pragmatic political form. Who put the concept on the table? There are always brilliant articles and speeches, but until ideas are gathered together at one focal point and put where it counts, in the committees of the Congress, they will have no impact. The key man in this regard was the chairman of the Senate Foreign Relations Committee, Arthur Vandenberg.

I never dreamed that Vandenberg would abandon isolationism altogether. As you know, he earlier had been notorious as a strong isolationist in the minds of people who had considered him their god. Marshall was crucial in the dealings with Vandenberg that resulted in legislation. But that's going too far ahead of myself.

The picture we often get is that while Marshall was in Russia, the bulk of the Marshall Plan speech was being written in Washington. There are certain crucial points that were being developed in Washington, but much of it never came together until after Marshall returned and made his speech about the failures of the Moscow Conference. At this time in late April 1947, Marshall called in Kennan and charged him with making a recommendation on American policy. Kennan had realized that he might be part of what Marshall considered to be his policy planning staff, having been told by Acheson in late January that he was being considered for the position. On the day Marshall took his oath of office, he told Acheson in effect, "I want a policy planning staff like the one I had in the Pentagon. I need some kind of committee where people can put their feet up and not think about reacting to today's cablegram or today's headlines, but about what comes six months from now, a year from now, something of the sort." Kennan, who was deputy commandant of the National War College, wanted to finish his tour that summer and was promised that he would be able to do that. Almost immediately, however, he was called on to help with other things in the State Department. He was on the committee which drew up the recommendations which were sent to Marshall and to the President that resulted in the Truman Doctrine Speech.

Now here is a question of evidence about which I don't know the answer. Flying back from Moscow, Marshall talked with Charles E. Bohlen and apparently wrote parts of his speech which he gave on 28 April. According to Bohlen's memoirs, Marshall kept wondering aloud how to save Europe economically, how to find initiatives which would prevent the Russians from reaping the benefits of Europe's economic demise. When I read Bohlen's language and when I talked to him in 1967 in Paris, I fear that he may have put into his recollections of what occurred on the way back from Moscow what he actually wrote into the draft of the Marshall Plan speech. Marshall's language may not have been quite that clear in his conversations with Bohlen. But Bohlen is partly right that Marshall was turning away from a discussion of what he had gone to Moscow to talk about, the business of settling the German treaty and, if possible, the Austrian treaty. He didn't really think he was going to get a German treaty. He told too many people that he didn't think he could. Both Senator Tom Connally and Senator Vandenberg of the Senate Foreign Relations Committee had told him that if he could get an Austrian Treaty that would be good, because it was going to take a long time to get everything settled.

This sequence is important to note because all kinds of historical necessities are satisfied by saying that Marshall somehow or another twisted the program for settling the German problem into the Marshall Plan. That isn't so. But if you put this problem of the treaties on hold, then you'll naturally talk about what's going to happen to the Western European countries that are in trouble. Before Marshall came home he had the added concern of the Truman Doctrine to deal with. Specifically, the fear was that if Greece and Turkey fell, what would happen to Italy and to France, and how would the pending elections in those two countries go?

In Marshall's mind there was immediate concern about the European economic situation. This was not something that he thought up; he at least knew about Europe's troubles from the Bevin *aide-mémoire*. He knew that Britain was running out of money and would not be able to carry out its commitments. So it is not surprising to find a shift from preoccupation with immediately settling the German and the Austrian treaties to addressing the question of what do we do in the next three or next six months. Bevin, who continually talked to Marshall in Moscow at noonday conferences, always said, "We need a special loan; we are running out of money; inflation is ruining us. We've got to have money before the end of the year." At the last meeting before Marshall left Moscow, Bevin told him he had to do something for France before the end of the year.

That was all in Marshall's mind. It was not something that he was told in Washington. I think these realizations prompted him, on the day after he returned from Moscow, to say to Acheson, "We have been talking about organizing this committee, as I asked you to do; now it's got to be activated." It was activated on the fifth of May. By that time Kennan, alerted by Acheson, and realizing that Marshall considered the Russians uninterested in solving Europe's economic chaos, had already asked for special papers, special documents on the situation in England, France, Austria, Germany, Italy, and two or three other Western European countries. So it wasn't a matter of him coming up with recommendations in a matter of two weeks. He had already been busily collecting papers and documents from various agencies.

It is important that Marshall get at least some credit at this point for giving the Marshall Plan momentum. The policy planning staff was going to produce some sort of a recommendation. But the plan was to come from Europe; we had no plan like the one that would come from Europe. What we did was request that Europe act and ask us for help.

Here is your first focus. There will be one or two more, and I think on these issues Marshall, as secretary of state, exercised his proper duties and had a hand in getting the focus set on what had to be done. Then he approached the man in the Senate who could get things done.

Kennan started work in an organized way with the committee on the fifth of May. Acheson told me—I think this is one of the cases where if he had had access to his State Department papers he might have made a slightly different statement—that there was no framework for the Marshall Plan recommendation until Clayton's 27 May memorandum. Yet if you look at the *Foreign Relations* volume you see that on the 15th of May the policy planning staff discussed certain general principles which were expanded into a temporary paper on which its report of 23 May drew. This paper even has some of the exact language that Bohlen put into the Marshall speech. From here came the statement that the initiative must come from Europe and that there must be two phases to the initiative: an interim program to aid those countries in desperate shape and a long-term program. The committee developed the idea that the initiative should be offered to all of Europe. This last suggestion, in particular, was Kennan's contribution.

The question I cannot answer is whether Marshall gave Kennan suggestions at this point. Marshall says that he didn't write the speech, but that there were two things which he insisted upon: that the offer be open to all European countries that agreed to work together and that the initiative must come from Europe. Whether he passed his feelings on to Kennan, I don't know. I do know that a week after Marshall returned from Moscow, he moved his office from the old State Department to a building that he and Henry Stimson had ordered built, which today is the old part of the new State Department. (It was built for the Army, and before it was finished Stimson said it wasn't big enough so they decided to begin that very summer on the present Pentagon.) Marshall saw to it that the office adjoining his was given to Kennan, and Kennan says in his memoirs—and in a memo that he handed me in 1967 before he wrote his memoirs—that Marshall encouraged him to come in whenever he had something to talk about and that he did avail himself of this opportunity. Whether any part of Marshall's feelings were fed into the speech or not I don't know. But I do know that there was an interplay between Marshall and the policy planning staff that early. The policy planning report wasn't something that Marshall suddenly saw for the first time on the 23rd of May.

Up until now we are dealing with material that is not focused absolutely on the immediacy of the problem. But on the 27th of May, Undersecretary of State Will Clayton returned from a meeting in Geneva with a memo which he brought to Acheson. Clayton requested that Acheson arrange a meeting with Marshall. I've never understood why he felt he had to go through Acheson because both worked at the undersecretary level. Anyway, Acheson thought the memo was dynamite. Marshall arranged for all upper level advisers to meet. He was obviously shaken. I think the specific effect of that memorandum was that it convinced Marshall that he couldn't wait any longer to make his initiative known. His first reaction, on the 28th or 29th of May, was to ask Acheson how it should be presented. He felt that it was important how the initiative was put before Congress and the people. Acheson's suggestion, after he had gone up to see several members of Congress, was that in several weeks Marshall should give a speech, making the public aware of the problem. A little later on, the President could make an official speech.

Two days later Marshall decided that he would make the speech at Harvard. I think everybody knows by now that marvelous sounding nonsense that Marshall simply rang up Harvard and said, "I just happened to remember, you offered me an honorary degree two years ago. Won't you give it to me now so I can come make a speech?" Then he went and spoke at the morning session when they hand out diplomas. That's not the way Harvard did things. They had offered him an honorary degree in 1945, but he hadn't thought it proper for him to be taking degrees when men were dying, so he turned it down. At that same time the next year he was in

China and was unable to accept the degree when it was offered again. The third year, 1947, he received another letter from President James Conant of Harvard saying in effect, "We'd like to offer you this degree again. You've got to come and get it. We won't give it to you *in absentia*. But will you come?" Marshall responded that he didn't know, he might be out of the country. In April, though, Conant received a letter from Marshall in which he said that he would come to accept a degree but that he wouldn't speak. But Conant hadn't asked him to speak; he asked him to accept an invitation from the head of the Alumni Association, Laird Bell. The main speeches at Harvard, apparently, are given in the afternoon session, but the morning session is handled by selected graduates with a little speech by the president. So Marshall initially didn't agree to make a speech. But on the 29th of May he wrote to Conant and said he could make a few remarks. I like that: "a few remarks." You can see the letter posted in the Marshall Library.

On the 30th, Marshall told General Carter, his political and military assistant, to get someone to write a less-than-ten-minute speech for him to give at Harvard. Marshall wanted the subject to be on economics, and he wanted to avoid a lot of passion. The speech would draw on the Kennan and Clayton reports and a short summary by Marshall. What is important is not who wrote the speech but who brought these reports together and focused them. Marshall made the decision as to what was to go into the speech. He made the decision to give the speech at Harvard, over the advice of the undersecretary, who said that nobody listens to commencement speeches, but that suited Marshall completely. He didn't want a big splash like the Truman Doctrine speech. He thought that that had gone overboard; he felt Truman had promised too much when we were not prepared to live up to the promise. He wanted his initiative kept relatively quiet. This is part of the reason why they didn't publicize it. The British were dumfounded that this speech wasn't played up.

Acheson, though, in his account forgot something. He claims that Marshall wrote the speech on the way to Harvard, and that he [Acheson] had to call "Pat" Carter and pry the thing out of Marshall. The impression you get is of Marshall writing as Lincoln was supposed to have done on the train to Gettysburg. The text of his speech was already in the State Department at four o'clock the day before he gave it, so it wasn't "pried out", and "Pat" Carter wasn't up there to be called. He didn't make the trip. Marshall went with General Omar Bradley. These are wonderfully dramatic words, but it shows that the man who recollects them wasn't in on that phase of things.

The two parts that were not in the speech that was distributed at the State Department on 4 June were the opening thanks and the final statement. Marshall had insisted on writing these parts. I don't think he wrote them out. At least I have found no text for them. The final statement is not the most beautiful piece of prose in the world. It gives every impression that he is summarizing the high points of everything he had just said, but in a less interesting way. If you listen to the speech you can see that this is the emotional part of it for him. He talks about something that the American people must do: it has to be done, it must be done. But the speech ends on an anticlimax; it would get a bad grade from a public speaking teacher.

As a matter of fact, people have claimed that Marshall mumbled through the entire speech. The tape doesn't show him mumbling, but it does show him being drowned out by planes. That part of the Harvard Yard where he spoke is within earshot of planes which are coming in or taking off from Logan Airport. You can understand why they didn't hear him very well.

Brad Perkins, who was one of those Harvard graduates, told me that he often tells his students of diplomacy that this shows how you can attend something and not know you've been to a historical event because he remembered the speech as rather dull. Then he claimed that he remembered some other man who made an even duller speech.

At any rate, Marshall made the speech and Bevin seized on it. Bevin and Bidault hoped that Molotov and the Soviets wouldn't come in, and they made it very clear that it would solve a lot of their problems if he didn't participate. Marshall and Kennan both said that they were inviting the Russians in good faith; Bohlen said that he never believed that the Russians would participate. Bohlen had one other point, with which I agree: he is correct that if the Russians had been in the plan, Congress would not have passed the necessary legislation.

Marshall was away attending three or four other meetings during the period of the framing of the plan in Paris. Robert A. Lovett, who succeeded Acheson as undersecretary of state at the end of June, on two occasions in answer to Sir Oliver Franks, the chairman of the European committee that had been set up in Paris to draft a plan, indicated that the committee had to stay put on what Marshall wanted, namely, that the initiative must come from Europe and the plan must come from Europe, but we could give friendly aid in framing the plan. The question, of course, was what the friendly aid would be. Twice Marshall intervened and issued a statement to encourage the Europeans, but at this stage you must give credit to a great number of people. It's important to notice these things, because if you read Acheson's memoirs, you would think that Acheson was in charge throughout the summer. He never says so, but people are aware of him setting up committees at the end of June, the one with Harriman for instance. Acheson claims that he went to General Marshall and asked him if he would persuade the President to set up these nonpartisan committees. But that was Vandenberg's idea, at least in part.

The recommendations of the plan from Europe were put into the form of legislation and introduced in the fall of 1947. That first legislation had to do with an interim appropriation of less than $1 billion. Marshall was one of the people who spoke for the committees. There was no real opposition to that amount of money for temporary aid in order to get the countries in the worst shape through until the following March. This legislation was passed on 15 December 1947, and two days later Truman, who had been holding back the main European Recovery Program (ERP), proposed that.

In early January Marshall set off on a two- or three-month period of what he called campaigning. As far as he was concerned, promoting European aid was just like running for president. He made speeches and appeared before committees and took part in activities to support the aid. Marshall, along with Lovett and one or two others, worked closely with the members of Congress. I don't think that opponents would ever have defeated some kind of aid legislation, because by this time there was a strong feeling in this country that something needed to be done. But the great fear was that it wouldn't be done quickly enough, and, secondly, that the legislation would be amended out of its original shape.

It is very interesting that Marshall, for the second time in five years, was *Time*'s "Man of the Year" in 1947. *Time* said that the one man who symbolized the will of the United States to help Europe, to lead Europe, was George Marshall. *Time* recognized the person who was giving the program to focus. Many people can make speeches, and you can read the speeches and they are very good, but the question is: Who is the man listening and who is the man that needs to listen? The main person in the committee, because of his leadership in the Republican party, was Vandenberg. You've got to remember that both houses were Republican, and that there were 20 or more hard-line Republican isolationists in the Senate. Bob Taft, the leading isolationist, was the second most powerful Republican in the Senate. But it was Marshall's and Lovett's day-to-day contact with Vandenberg which was crucial. It was kept very quiet, being handled at Blair House. Their strategy kept things on the road in the Senate. Again and again, the approach would be worked out between the three of them, and Vandenberg would go out and make the fight, and he was able to get the vote of his own party. Truman was holding the Democrats pretty much in line.

Concerning Marshall's speeches, I think he enjoyed making them as much as anything in his life. If you listen to the tapes you can tell he took great satisfaction from his speaking. He spoke in Pittsburgh up in his own bailiwick; he spoke in Atlanta to the cotton growers and tobacco farmers; he spoke to a Des Moines convention via telephone after he was forced down in Knoxville by a storm; he made two speeches out on the West Coast. When it looked as if John Taber was going to cut the appropriation badly, Marshall decided to get the women's clubs into the act. He went to Portland and spoke to their national conference. Perhaps he exaggerated the impact that these women had by passing resolutions in all their chapters in an effort to influence enough votes to kill Taber's action, but he believed that they were crucial. Even so, Marshall accepted Vandenberg's decision to accept a plan from Republicans in the House that would cut this appropriation by making it apply for 15 months instead of 12, thus in effect cutting it that much unless it was found that it was needed in 12. Of course, in a short time it was found to be needed in 12.

I think if you follow that story you will see that Marshall certainly had a definite part in making the speech and in the philosophy of the speech. It is interesting that the Nobel speech goes back again to this same notion that the United States has to take a world position of leadership, that we cannot go back into isolation because we are the only country with the power to give this leadership, and that we cannot give it up. I think that is the essence of what was done.

QUESTION: Do you think it would be a good idea for us now to be developing something like the Marshall Plan to aid our Latin American neighbors who are in severe economic distress?

MR. POGUE: You have to have countries and governments that are going concerns, that are able to do something for themselves. The essence of the success of the Marshall Plan was the fact that Europe needed somebody to get them off dead center. They needed hope—that word comes up again and again and was mentioned by Kennan and picked up immediately by Marshall. What is forgotten is that Europe by 1946 had already made some progress, but it was losing momentum as fast as they could generate it. There had to be some kind of European unity. Whether or not the Latin American states now provide that possibility, I don't know, but I doubt it. As to whether it's a good idea, I would say yes. But I don't think you can expect the same results just by announcing a Marshall-type plan. It has also been suggested for the Far East and again, that was the main topic of discussion in that 1967 meeting in Brussels. As far as a replica of the Marshall Plan is concerned, it wouldn't work because everything would have to be on a larger scale.

QUESTION: Could you explain Acheson's intervention in the episode in the White House when Marshall was reading the statement about aid to Greece and Turkey? Wasn't that connected with Marshall's speech?

MR. POGUE: The subject on which Acheson claims he saved the day when Marshall flubbed it was on Greece and Turkey. Marshall went with Acheson to a meeting at the White House concerning Greece and Turkey in February, long before the Marshall Plan speech was made. I think Acheson exaggerates his role there for these reasons. The statement in *Foreign Relations* that Marshall was reading to members of Congress was written by Acheson, Loy Henderson, and other members of the hard-line school. It expounded the domino theory: If Greece and Turkey go, Italy goes; if Italy goes, France goes. Acheson said Marshall didn't scare them enough; it scares me to read that! Now maybe Marshall didn't read very loudly, maybe he didn't read it with any "aggression," but it is in that

statement and it says in *Foreign Relations*—and I've read the
original—that this statement was prepared for Marshall to
read at the White House meeting. And he read it! I suggest
that what Acheson did was add the "rousements." There is an
old joke about the rural preacher, that he never said anything
in his sermon but he added powerful "rousements." Acheson
was something of a courtroom lawyer, and I imagine he added
rousement too. Acheson has this problem; you've got to
watch him throughout. Of course his version was accepted by
Joseph Jones in *Fifteen Weeks*, but I've gathered that Jones
was not at that conference and that he got his information
from Acheson, then Acheson quotes Joe Jones as his source.
You don't have two sources; you don't really even have one,
which is a very different thing. I suspect the follow-up speech
somebody alludes to is the Delta Council speech. It had
nothing to do with the Harvard speech.

I didn't have time to go out to see Vandenberg's papers
at Ann Arbor, but I had a fellow there who had worked for
me earlier do a little work in the files. This person found no
evidence that Vandenberg said anything about Acheson's
statement, and I would think he'd remember saying something
like, "How marvelous, marvelous, marvelous. If you say that
to the American people, it will pass right away." Vandenberg
never wrote anything like that. My colleague found two
documents in the file for that period; both are copies of the
statement that Marshall read. Whoever edited the
Vandenberg diaries, either his son or the man who helped
him, says that it was Marshall who moved these people. I
don't think Acheson would make that up; I think that he did
put some embellishments in. I think the statement Marshall
read was basically written by Loy Henderson, although when
it came to the tough rhetoric of the Truman Doctrine speech
some of that was added by Clark Clifford. You can see all
the notes that are written back and forth between Clifford and
George Elsey in the Truman Library. The funny thing,
though, about that first draft Loy Henderson wrote—and he is

one of the hardest of hard-liners—was that it was described by a White House staff member as tame.

QUESTION: What was the dollar amount of the Marshall aid? Was it in the form of loans or grants?

MR. POGUE: They were mainly grants. The big thing that Kennan said in the beginning was that we could not fool around with any more loans; we've got to give grants, and we should give as much as we can. We should go ahead with the loans that were already talked about. The actual amount comes to approximately $13.5 billion. But I've heard four or five briefings—in the White House or State Department or elsewhere—in which that earlier figure has now reached an equivalent of $100 billion. I've heard the secretary of state say $60 billion or something like that. The next week it seems when the President spoke, or the secretary of the treasury spoke, they added another ten billion. But you've got to keep in mind, of course, that we had a defense budget of $15 billion at that time. Whatever the figure, the sum wasn't chicken feed.

QUESTION: I wonder, Forrest, if I may read one of the many fascinating sentences on Marshall from the fourth volume and ask you to give us a comment on it. "Although totally opposed to communism, he was the last important American leader to conclude that the Soviets preferred prolonging world chaos to making peace." What were the decisive factors that led the general to change his assessment?

MR. POGUE: I think basically it was the realization that it wasn't just Molotov giving him all the trouble. He kept thinking that Molotov does not accept anything; he is just sitting there saying "*nyet, nyet, nyet,*" inflating the same arguments over and over again. Of course you can look at it the other way and say that Marshall was being stubborn.

Anyway, Marshall had always had the notion that if you could get to Stalin and get him to make a promise, and if he understood that he had made a promise, then he would keep his word. Marshall hadn't gone to see Stalin when he first went to Moscow, but then he exercised his privilege as a guest and told Bedell Smith to arrange a meeting with Stalin. Marshall opened the meeting very forthrightly and told Stalin that during the war and immediately afterwards, he had had the goodwill of the United States. He was popular; but by the actions of Molotov and others he was losing that popularity. Stalin responded that the United States hadn't kept its word on certain things either. They continued to tell him that reparations were not good, but Stalin said his people thought they were very good. Then Marshall would protest that the foreign ministers were adjourning without coming to any agreement. Stalin said that these were just skirmishes, the first round in a long battle, and when we exhaust ourselves, then we'll make a deal. In Marshall's and Bohlen's minds, Stalin did not want to settle any problem in Germany or Austria at that time. If the economic chaos continued, it would be in Russia's interest, and Marshall became convinced of this after that meeting.

Harriman had said in three or four speeches before this, that Marshall was the one man who held out hope of negotiating any sort of settlement. That comes directly out of a statement Marshall made to me. He told me that Harriman always said that you cannot negotiate with these people but that he kept trying. He defensively said, "I thought we ought to try it, and I think the American people thought we should talk to them."

QUESTION: Doesn't it depend on how you look at the terms of the negotiations? In fact, during that very negotiation in Moscow, some of the Americans—particularly General Lucius Clay—felt definitely that an agreement could result from the negotiations, depending upon what you offered the Soviets. This was particularly true with regard to reparations from current production, and only after a tremendous struggle between Dulles and Clay did Marshall finally decide in favor of Dulles's general view. The American position was one in which the Russians would not get much in the way of reparations from current production and would be excluded from any participation in supervising production in the Ruhr. On those conditions the prospects for any settlement were almost inconceivable. What are your views on that?

MR. POGUE: I think that Clay at times was not as convinced of all this as he appears to be because he shows quite a bit of ambiguity about what he had in mind. I know the historian John Gunbel brings up part of this. The Russians were more agreeable than the French on many issues; he blames the French. At a conference at the Marshall Library, in which I did the commentary, Jean Smith said that they picked Marshall because he was a hard-liner. That is absurd. They picked him because Truman needed somebody of stature to succeed Byrnes. He was not picked as a hard-liner. Jean said that same day that Bedell Smith was picked by Marshall as ambassador, and of course that isn't so. But before Marshall left for Moscow he told Connally and Vandenberg, "I'm being briefed three or four hours a day and certain things can be dealt with and certain other things cannot; they are non-negotiable."

QUESTION: I'd like to change the focus a little bit. Could you assess the relative responsibilities of Bevin and Marshall with regard to the origins of the North Atlantic Treaty?

MR. POGUE: There seems to be no doubt, if you read Lord Gladwyn Jebb's memoirs, that he had prepared a paper indicating that Bevin was thinking about it when he talked to Marshall in December 1947. There is a memo from 17 December, to the effect that Bevin was working on such a treaty. Marshall went to tell Bevin goodbye and Bevin threw out a general concept. That isn't an exact account of what took place, but Bevin came up with the concept first.

NARRATOR: If there are any lessons of a broader kind, it seems to me that the first is that individuals count. You have proved that, Dr. Pogue. Incidentally, Marshall, who always called people by their last name called Forrest Pogue, Dr. Pogue, because he had a great respect for the role of intellectuals.

MR. POGUE: I don't think that he was indicating that I was in favor of that. I admit I wasn't as close to him as those he called by their last name. But he did feel that he had been poorly educated, and he'd stop right in the middle of something to ask me, "I never did understand the difference between these two words. Would you explain that to me?" He wasn't being playful at all; he wanted to know and was quite willing to ask. He had a wonderful intellectual curiosity. I said in the first book that he had the curiosity of an intellectual or a scholar, but he never had the time or the inclination to pursue it. He was forever asking why.

My favorite story is in the fourth volume. Marshall suddenly realized he had been put in charge of the Manhattan Project, yet he didn't know what an atom was. He thought he should find out so he had them bring up a whole library cart of books. He read all afternoon and suddenly realized the war would be over before he learned. So he thought he had to find somebody who knew about atoms and trust him. Of course Leslie Groves didn't know either, but Leslie knew if somebody told him something should be done he would go and pound on somebody's desk and it would be done. Groves told me that Admiral King decided he had better learn something about atoms too. So he sent for encyclopedias and then raised hell because they didn't contain some of the new terms such as fission. That stopped him cold.

The other point concerns Marshall's reading. He read omnivorously but it was the most oddly prolix batch of books you ever saw. When he was a colonel, General McCoy was appointed to the Lytton Commission, which as you remember went to China for the League of Nations. He told Marshall to put together a reading list. Marshall's list contained some of the things that any of us who are students of diplomacy would mention. But he also listed Harold Lamb's *Genghis Khan*, marvelous reading but devoid of any facts. I imagine he liked those best. And then he said if you want to understand India, which indirectly affects China, read *Mother India* by Katherine Mayo, which is not highly esteemed for its scholarship.

NARRATOR: Maybe all of you understood the point about the Truman Doctrine, but the plain fact is that practically all of us who have written on the Cold War have tended to take the Acheson explanation at face value, which I even thought I had seen one time in Vandenberg's memoirs. I don't know whether I saw it in Harriman's book, but I saw it in various places. Their thesis was that Marshall was too vague and general, and Vandenberg turned on him and told him that he had to be much tougher or the Congress wouldn't accept this at all. And then Acheson gave the opposite kind of a speech. All of us who have been writing about this problem had taken that view as gospel. Pogue's interpretation, even though somebody may some day prove that even Forrest Pogue didn't have the whole truth, is one of the reasons scholars go to the sources.

MR. POGUE: I might add to this that Marshall continued to insist that you have to understand that it is human beings who are deciding and you must understand the background. He said to me at the outset of my work, "I don't care what you say about me, but before you write, find out what I knew at the time, what the climate of opinion was, and what I had to deal with. Then write what you like." And I think he meant it.

CHAPTER 8

The Rhetoric and Reality of Change in the Soviet Union*

GENERAL GEORGE M. SEIGNIOUS II

NARRATOR: General George Seignious has had an absolutely remarkable military career and has emerged as a kind of soldier-statesman. He rose in rank from second lieutenant to lieutenant general. He was commanding officer of the 44th Tank Brigade, 1951-52; assistant executive secretary of the Joint Chiefs of Staff, 1952-55; training adviser in Spain, 1956-57; executive to the secretary of the United States Army, 1957-60. In the 1960s he was commanding officer of the 11th Calvary, chief of staff of the Third Armored Division, Federal Republic of Germany; director of policy planning, office of the Secretary of Defense; assistant commander, 2nd Infantry Division, Korea; deputy director of plans and policy, Joint Chiefs of Staff; military adviser to the Paris Peace Talks; and commanding general, 3d Infantry Division, Federal Republic of Germany. In the 1970s he was United States commander in Berlin; deputy chief U.S. Mission in Berlin; deputy assistant secretary of defense in charge of military assistance and sales; director of the Defense Security

---

Presented in a Forum at the Miller Center on 13 March 1989.

Assistance Agency; director, Joint Chiefs of Staff Organization, Joint Chiefs of Staff; president of the Citadel; delegate-at-large to the SALT talks in Geneva; and delegate-at-large and director of ACDA. Until recently, he has been president of the Atlantic Council.

During his career, General Seignious has received a Distinguished Service Medal with two oak-leaf clusters, the Silver Star, the Bronze Star with two oak-leaf clusters, the Legion of Merit with three oak-leaf clusters, and numerous other awards.

Recently he was sent to the Soviet Union with General Scowcroft and General Goodpaster, among others, and looked at the subject of change in the Soviet Union. It is therefore entirely appropriate and fitting that that should be the subject we address today. It's a great honor to have you with us, General.

GENERAL SEIGNIOUS: Thank you, Ken. After that recitation, I'm exhausted. It does remind me of a wonderful British story. Two elderly British gentlemen who had been lifelong friends hadn't seen each other for years. They met in their London club to reminisce about old friends and incidents that they had shared. After an hour, they couldn't remember a name or an incident, and they were completely exhausted. One turned to the other and said, "I'm exhausted. We'd better stop this." The other one said, "I'm certainly glad you said that, but before we go would you tell me whether it was you or your brother who was killed in World War II?"

If everything Mr. Gorbachev is declaring in rhetoric comes true, the entire structure for world peace as we have known it for the last 50 years will change substantially. It's a tough proposition, as this new hue is being woven to the tapestry, to know exactly what that final tapestry will look like. The certainty of Mr. Gorbachev's sincerity, I think, is upon us. The certainty of where this will all come out is not upon us, so it is up to you and to me to begin a serious analysis of what it takes to build the confidence necessary for us to alter or change the policy direction that we've been engaged in all of this time.

We certainly don't want to make changes prematurely. We do not want to do what Genscher in Germany is doing, engaging in euphoria as if the millennium has arrived. But neither do we want to be such cynical obstructionists that we impede an opportunity for change in the Soviet Union that could in years to come be fundamental.

The history of the use of force has changed remarkably through the years. When Alexander came out of Macedonia—I think it was 343 B.C.—he used force to gain wealth for his empire. That practice continued up through the 20th century; empires were built on the use and deployment of force. The British empire was built in large measure due to its capacity to use force for the acquisition of wealth for their nation.

Since nuclear weapons have come along, superpowers face a great risk in using force even for intimidation. We have seen, since World War II, that the destructive power of modern weapons—both nuclear and conventional—has changed the dimensions of war and the risks undertaken when people intrude in other territories where they are unwelcome. The capacity to acquire wealth with the use of force has diametrically changed. In fact, we are in a coincidence in history, I think, where both superpowers realize that the use of large structures of military force is depleting wealth to the point where there must be some form of accommodation. I think Gorbachev has arrived at that, and I think it has been our position as a defensive nation since World War II that we would welcome a lessening of military confrontation around the world. If he is sincere in his objectives, then we can proceed on that basis.

What did we hear in Moscow? Brent Scowcroft, Andy Goodpaster, and others, all experienced negotiators and experienced men in international affairs, were on the team with me. We arrived at the conclusion that Gorbachev is sincere, and sincere in his own self-interest, not because he is a sweet man. He has got to change, or the Soviet Union will be literally a third-class power.

The Soviets told us some astounding things, and I thought I would take from my notes four or five of the comments that were made to us by our interlocutors as the basis for our assumption that this is serious business we're in, not just polemics and propaganda.

(1) Under new thinking in the Soviet Union, they no longer will export socialism to any other country or export revolution to any other country. (Mind you, throughout these notes I'm telling you what I heard. Don't shoot the messenger if you don't believe it. We'll try to interpret it together.)

(2) The countries of Eastern Europe have the freedom to choose their own social and economic courses, without direction or interference from the Soviet Union.

(3) Gorbachev's people said, "You've all heard what Mr. Gorbachev has said about the concept of a common European home, meaning that each nation in central Europe has a right to live in a common home, have their own apartment, and not have intrusion from their neighbors." The thing that astounded us was that they said, "The United States is entitled to have an apartment in that common home, and furthermore the Soviet Union wants the United States in that common home, because you add a degree of stability that we wouldn't have otherwise." (One should read into that a bit of German influence and the need for a stabilized and, I would say, nonreunified Germany.) They further said that they had no intent under their new thinking to divide the United States from their allies in central Europe, again, with this viewpoint of stability.

(4) Under their new thinking, they say it has been determined that Soviet goals and Soviet aspirations cannot in today's world be achieved by the use of military force. As a parallel to that, a central purpose of the Soviet Union now is to find ways of reaching stability, particularly in the confrontation between the Warsaw Pact and NATO. They

believe that the current relationship and structure is superfluous, excessively expensive, and irrational.

In explaining to us what this new Soviet military doctrine of "reasonable sufficiency" means, they placed very high emphasis on the difference in military doctrine between the Soviet Union and in the Western world. The military doctrine of the Soviet Union, according to them, is a basic part of their political philosophy and doctrine. In other words, it's the centerpiece to the political management of their country. The military implementation of it has normally been left to the Soviet general staff in the past, that the entire doctrine itself is an integral part of the political philosophy of the nation. We can develop that more in the discussion period.

We really took them to task on why it is that they keep talking about this reasonable sufficiency, and yet have their tank factories, gun factories, ship factories, and aircraft factories continuing to turn out the same volume of material that they have for the last three years. We said, "Under Gorbachev you haven't changed the production cycles. Why is it, then, that you say you are going for reasonable sufficiency? This is an unreasonable level. You are turning out 280 tanks a month. That's enough to arm one tank division per month, and more than we in the Western world turn out in a year, or at least in six months. Why is it, then, that you keep your forces deployed right up to the border of NATO? You haven't withdrawn a single tank [at that time]. What do you mean? How do you think you can, by rhetoric, persuade those of us in the West who have had our minds set for 40 years, to suddenly alter our whole doctrinal concept, our whole perception of what the Soviet Union is, when you are only dealing in rhetoric and not deeds?"

Well, they were a little taken aback by that straightforward question. They answered it in a calm way, and there was no acrimony about it. They said, "The five-year plan that controls our production for military hardware and the entire command economy of the Soviet Union does not run out until 1991." They said that with a straight face. They said, "We haven't yet figured out how to convert a tank factory into a tractor factory. We haven't figured out the management skills that have to be shifted. We don't even know, frankly, what our defense budget is. We don't have the statistics to back it up."

The chief of the Red Army, in a private conversation with a member of our delegation, said the same thing. He said, "If I need 1,500 trucks or a 1,000 tanks, I order them. I do not have a budget for the Red Army." In further explanation they said: "We tried six months ago to examine the economic and political impact of altering the 1991 five-year defense plan, and we couldn't get to first base because we don't know how to do it. It's just like the British trying to move from driving in the left lane to driving in the right lane; they didn't know how to do it all at once, so they decided the first two months all the automobiles would be shifted over, and then two months later the lorries would be shifted over . . ." and he raised his arms and said, "You know what a disaster that would be! That's the same thing we're faced with."

They will now have to face up to it, and that's when we will see some tangible indicators to go along with some of the unilateral declarations on military force. We do know that some transportation units are being used in the Ukraine for the distribution of foodstuff to the central cities. Their distribution system is abominable. They raise a lot of grain and a lot of things to eat, but they can't get it from where it's raised to where it's consumed. The spoilage rate is fantastic; they have neither the refrigeration nor the system for distribution.

I've been told that a tank factory has been converted to a tractor factory, but that's only one out of hundreds. How long it will be before we see the productive resources of the Soviet Union turn to domestic requirements such as housing, medical attention, and food, I'm not so sure.

It is a stagnated society economically and socially. It has such insuperable internal political obstacles to overcome, that

I wouldn't give Mr. Gorbachev a high chance of success in perestroika. I think there will be progress, but whether it will meet the expectations of the people in time to retain political stability in the country, I don't know. I don't know whether this is true or not, but it is a good story. When Gorbachev was here in December and met with Mr. Reagan and Mr. Bush up at the Statue of Liberty, a reporter got to him and asked, "Mr. General Secretary, what are the chances of perestroika succeeding?" Gorbachev allegedly turned to him and said, "Jesus Christ doesn't know that answer." I think that was a pretty good way of putting it.

Staying in an ecclesiastical context, this whole process is at Ash Wednesday, not Easter. What we need to do as a nation is to begin planning contingently what our vision is if Easter comes. We should prudently plan now for a structure of forces within the alliance, so that step by step, as we gain confidence that real events are taking place, we will know what we want. We don't want 16 nations of Europe to plan independently for what *they* want our strategy to be, what *they* want our force structure to be. We should set some goals, and we haven't. The President, Brent Scowcroft, and Secretary Baker have formed a planning team for setting some goals for a NATO summit meeting which will take place, as I understand it, on 29 May. They have a very short deadline to come up with some major decisions, not only on conventional forces, but also on naval and strategic nuclear forces. We are at that coincidence in history when the resources to be applied to our military structure in face of our national deficit will inevitably go down probably to zero-growth budget levels—at least that is what is forecasted within the Beltway.

I don't think our current force structure is sustainable, particularly at the levels of the early Reagan years. Something has to give, and we want to be sure that we are prudently dealing with these budgetary pressures.

The unilateral proposals of Mr. Gorbachev in his speech at the United Nations on 7 December were stunning. They were well thought out, and there was a conceptual context to them. Let me give you one illustration. He said, "All right, we'll reduce 5,000 tanks from East Germany, Czechoslovakia, and Hungary. We will reduce 10,000 tanks overall; we'll reduce 50,000 people out of those three countries; and we'll have an overall reduction of 500,000."

This addressed almost every point of the search for credibility that we've been seeking—in a small way, yes, and not in a way that will change the strategic balance. Let me illustrate this. If he takes six tank divisions beginning next month out of those three countries—and Honecker has already announced that four of them will come out of East Germany—that leaves one to come out of Hungary and one out of Czechoslovakia to meet the six. If you do that, you take out a total of 2,000 tanks. Those tank formations in East Germany are the most threatening to us as far as time and space is concerned. So, it is of significance that four of the six come out of Germany, which is closest and most threatening to us.

Second, if you are taking out 5,000 tanks and only 2,000 are in those six divisions, where are the other 3,000? Those will come from the other Soviet divisions that are stationed there, and the removal of tank elements from those divisions gives credibility to Gorbachev's statement that his remaining forces will become much more defensive in character. If he removes the artillery and the tanks from those structures, it gives credibility to the fact that the others are shifting in their mission to a more defensive structure.

Thus, there are many encouraging signs, and if the West can hold cohesively together for a couple of years, I think that the hue in the fabric of the tapestry that I mentioned when I started will become clearer, the hope for peace will grow, and we might have finally arrived at a posture where the structure for peace in the world will be much more stable. Then the enormous resources that have been spent in the last 50 years can be spent elsewhere, and we will be moving progressively, I hope, from Ash Wednesday to Easter.

QUESTION: What took NATO so long to enter the arms negotiations?

GENERAL SEIGNIOUS: On 9 December, NATO put out its communique on its starting position for the conventional arms talk; it was a singularly unimaginative document. They were talking in terms of a 5 percent or a maximum of 10 percent reduction in NATO forces to match the declarations by the Soviets to go to parity and then down to an equal level. They also stated in the document that it would not be NATO to Warsaw Pact negotiation; it would be individual national delegations, 16 from NATO and seven from the East. That came about because of the French. I'm going to say some very straightforward things about that, because the French have been our allies most of the time for many years. They are engaged in a vision, in my opinion, that is likely to be divisive, particularly for U.S. national interests. I say that for the following three or four reasons.

First, they insist on a philosophy of negotiating outside of a pact or an alliance structure. Because of the historical Gaullist view of "the Atlantic to the Urals," they want to see French influence become preeminent again in dealing with central European countries. That's quite a harsh statement about our friends, but I think in intellectual circles in France they have this image of themselves playing a greater role for France, particularly in dealing with central Europe.

Secondly, the French are very opposed to any constraints on the modernization of their nuclear weapons. Right now, they know of the great debate going on in West Germany about the modernization of the Lance system, a potentially very divisive element of our alliance relationships. But the French pronounced the other day that they are going full steam ahead on developing a Hades mid-range nuclear system. Maybe that's not all bad militarily, but I don't want the security of the United States dependent on French nuclear decisions.

Thirdly, they have taken the lead in trying to revitalize the Western European Union (WEU), which is a union of twelve Western European nations from which the United States is excluded. The French have taken the lead role in trying to organize it, and they rationalize it as strengthening the second pillar of the Western alliance. This is fine if it's kept within the context of the alliance and the cohesiveness of the alliance, but there are signals that the French are trying to gain so much power that it will diminish the power of the United States. In due course, I think we will see a diminished role for the United States in the alliance. But what I am pleading for is to not do it too soon, because if by congressional action we demand that we withdraw 100,000 troops because the burden sharing isn't equitable, we will begin to unravel something that has been cohesive and has been the strength of our political, economic, and military position for 40 years. And goodness knows what happens when 1992 comes and the Common Market goes into flower. Here again, we have the French leading all kinds of actions in the commercial and economic sense, which exclude, for the moment at least, American corporations.

I urge you to try to read what some French are thinking. I don't think they have the clout to pull it off, but we should pay attention to their position. I was talking to a European diplomat on Friday and I said, "You know, I'm concerned about some of these indications, and I don't think our French friends are being realistic. I think it's too idealistic for them to think like this." He said, "They are thinking more than that. They want you out of there." I don't go quite that far. I don't think they are trying to drive the United States out of Western Europe, but I do think they are not thinking clearly about how badly cohesion is needed in the alliance, at least as we are perceived through this uncertain period with the Soviet Union. That's a long answer to a very good question.

QUESTION: Do we have a planning structure in place in our military-political circles to enable the administration to come up with any sort of a responsible and significant position at the meeting in May you referred to?

GENERAL SEIGNIOUS: I think the need is recognized, and I think the President gave direction to his advisers, Brent Scowcroft and the secretary of state, that he wanted such a plan. But it has been delayed in getting substance to it because of the uncertainties in the Defense Department. The structure in the Defense Department is not in place. We will probably see all of the deputy secretaries that Tower had selected change. There has been an impediment to proper planning within our national government in the last 45 to 50 days.

I have confidence that we will come up with a plan that sets out some goals. I know at the Atlantic Council we are going to publish a paper. We've already sent it to the President, and it was signed by General Goodpaster, who was a former supreme allied command to Europe and one of General Eisenhower's closest advisers. The paper calls for, among other things, a concept and a plan that will gain the support and keep the support of the parliaments and the Congress and people of the United States, so that we don't begin preemptive unilateral withdrawals on an untimely basis. General Goodpaster said, "It would add to the security of both NATO and the United States if we had a goal of reducing down to 50 percent of what NATO is now structured for, provided each step is matched by a Soviet reduction that would take them down to 50 percent of the current NATO level, which means that the Soviet Union and the Warsaw Pact would have to reduce by almost 80 percent in order to come down to parity."

The notion is of a structure of forces reconfigured, as long as we could reenforce it with adequate warning. Thus, if the Warsaw Pact forces in question are pulled back and disbanded and destroyed, we thereby enhance and increase the warning time that would accompany any attempt at recreating an ability for a surprise attack. We would have time to react, but it would take a considerable restructuring of our forces to do so.

QUESTION: Have we offered any kind of plan for helping the Russians start manufacturing tractors and trucks instead of all of these tanks, helping them reconvert to peaceful uses?

GENERAL SEIGNIOUS: No we haven't.

QUESTION: Why not?

GENERAL SEIGNIOUS: Because they don't want it in the first place. They want credits; they want money; and they want technology. They know that any Western country would be on the margin of trying to enhance or make more efficient the perestroika endeavors of Mr. Gorbachev.

But there is another point. When Chancellor Kohl went to Moscow in October, he took 50-odd businessmen, and all of them were passing out lines of credit like nothing mattered. Well, tied credits—tied to medical facilities or tied to agricultural productions—would be one thing; but simply doling out lines of untied credit before this thing solidifies a little bit is pretty tricky business. Who knows how those lines of credit will be used or what they'll buy?

COMMENT: They won't let our businessmen go over there, for instance. Maybe somebody from the Ford Motor Company could go over and show them how we reconverted after World War II.

GENERAL SEIGNIOUS: The Soviets have offered very complex procedures by which Western businesses could go in and gain a 49 percent ownership in a production facility within the Soviet Union, but that's not too attractive to people who are profit oriented, because the ruble is nonconvertible. When we were there, we had to pay $1.60 for one lousy ruble, and people would come up to us on the street and say, "We'll give you seven rubles for every dollar you give us." It's very illegal, and we didn't do it, but that's a difference between $1.60 and $0.20. What businessman is going into the Soviet Union on a joint venture when he doesn't know how he will get his profits or anything else out?

There is a little motion in that direction. Surprisingly, the Turks are moving into some parts of Southern Russia. The Japanese, the Germans, and the Swiss are also interested. Ten American corporations are working on joint ventures in the Soviet Union. Kendall, from Pepsi Cola, made the smartest move several years ago. Knowing this hard-currency problem, he said, "I'll tell you what I'll do. I'll set up Pepsi Cola factories for you and manufacture all the Pepsi Colas the Russians want to drink, provided you give me exclusive rights to import a certain kind of vodka into the United States." So Kendall is manufacturing Pepsi like hell in the Soviet Union, importing a very good brand of vodka into this country, and you are buying it. He's making a profit at both ends.

QUESTION: My question involves your observations as to whether Gorbachev can pull off what he's postulating. I've got two vignettes. The first is that we were riding in a train several years ago between Leningrad and Moscow. Our tourist guide was a young woman whose husband was a naval architect, and we shared something in our background. We talked for almost the entire trip. She was very interested in Mr. Jefferson, and I responded to the extent that I could about him. One observation that I made to her was that based on Mr. Jefferson's history in this country, if you open the window (pointing to the window of the train) just a little bit and you let in ideas of freedom, you don't know where this will lead you as a country.

The second vignette comes from a talk I had with Irving R. Levine at a dinner about two years ago. He had been a correspondent in Moscow, and his observation about Mr. Gorbachev in the context then was that Gorbachev had a very short window of time to pull off what he was postulating;

otherwise, events would overcome him. I think it's curious that folks in this country in general think that the Soviet Union is a monolithic country; of course, it is not. I would be interested, in terms of the people that you spoke to in the Soviet Union, whether you thought that he did have the ability as a leader to pull off the things that he has proposed. Do you have any thought about the amount of time that he had to do this in?

GENERAL SEIGNIOUS: There is no question that there is full evidence that glasnost is working at full steam. Soviet television and Soviet newspapers, including *Izvestia* and the whole range of what we used to think were official newspapers, are printing highly critical articles about life in the Soviet Union. The absence of medical treatment and food—and I can say food five times and couldn't emphasize it enough—is the thing that is liable to cause a loss of political control more than any other one thing.

But the fact of the matter is that you are quite correct in saying that if you open the window, and Mr. Jefferson was certainly right in this country, that you get rising expectations and a ventilation of what the truth really is, versus controlled information. I really don't believe that he can put that genie back in the bottle, and I don't mean just Gorbachev. I mean anybody that succeeds him; without the most repressive, brutal regime in the history of mankind, more suppressive and brutal than Stalin, that genie cannot be put back. I think the chances of a complete reversion to neo-Stalinism are small and become smaller with each passing six or seven months.

I'm not wise enough—and I don't think that I know anybody who is—to give a time table on when expectations and when ethnic and racial problems in the regions of the Soviet Union reach such a point that it will cause Mr. Gorbachev to be removed. I will say to you that I think he is on a very high risk course. I think he is probably the most intelligent and flexible leader the Soviet Union has had since Lenin; I think he is a Leninist. I think he is an adversary of the most adroit dimensions as far as we are concerned. If he stays on his current course, I think it's best for us and our interests for him to succeed, at least in the short term. I can't say that we should be pulling against him, but I don't think we should be pulling for him to the point where we as a nation are relying on him and are willing to run risks in the change of our policies. I don't think we've got the degree of certainty to provide untied credits or to provide technology. I do think that events in the Soviet Union will never be the same, and our current ambassador, Jack Matlock, thinks that this man is changing the political structure of the Soviet Union fast enough that he will be able to keep control at least for the foreseeable future. Therefore, I suspect he'll survive for quite some time.

QUESTION: I was really indeed heartened at one of your opening comments that we are at a turning point, a changing point right now. Some decisions are going to be made for rather significant, maybe even drastic, changes in direction. I feel that the United States is in the most critical time ever in its history right now. A continuation of the old Cold War would be utterly disastrous. We have a fantastic opportunity. I only wish that we had come up with the invention of the change in direction, and not let Mr. Gorbachev do so. I think it's not too late for us to steal some of the initiative and come back to him one better.

One of the feelings I think in recent years has been meshing out fiscal policy with our foreign policy, and they seem to have been going off in very diverse opposite directions. You mentioned pulling out troops from Europe as an example. We have our preferences, but the fiscal facts are such that we are deeply constrained. This year our spending is going to be $283 billion over and above our income, stealing out of the trust fund and so forth. By 1993 that total of overspending will amount to $4 trillion, just eight years to go. I think we're in a contest here as to which comes first, an economic collapse or a failure to take advantage of the opportunities to reduce this arms burden. Are we finally in Washington going to look at the whole thing as an integrated problem, and take an integrated strategy—diplomatic, military economic—and package something that is workable and will solve our economic problems as well as these threats of annihilation that we've had hanging over our head?

GENERAL SEIGNIOUS: I would hope so. I think that integration of economic and security policy is one of the voids at the seat of government and has been for some time, and there are thoughtful people concerned about it.

I want to put in perspective two things that you said. You said you hoped that we could take some of the initiatives of Mr. Gorbachev and gain the initiative ourselves. I think that's an important point, but I also want to make the point that Gorbachev is responding to *our* initiatives. These are the goals that we've been trying to get the Soviets to accomplish for the last 40 years. I know he has the identity in Western Europe, and I know he has the image of coming forward with all these initiatives, but this is what the West has been calling for. Now we have to upstage that, if you will, and go for something so that the parliaments and the Congress will give us more time to make this adjustment as far as the military is concerned.

We are not running these deficits solely because of military expenditures. Our military expenditures are under 6 percent of our gross national product compared to Korea days or to Vietnam days. The overall allocation of what we are spending on military as opposed to what we are spending on social services is as low as it has been in, I think, 20-odd years.

Let me close the question this way, because part of this is related to a very critical issue called "burden sharing." Many people in the Congress are saying, "Why is it that we are still spending 6 percent of our GNP on military forces and Japan is spending 1 percent; Denmark, 2.2 percent; and Canada, 1.4 percent?"

We think that comprehensive security is a wonderful way to look at it, integrated with economics. One of our great problems is getting a more level playing field with Japan. The Atlantic Council not long ago started a program in Japan where we tried to do just this, saying, "Okay, we know that you are spending 1 percent of your GNP on defense. We also know that you are buying a self-defense force that gives you the third largest defense budget in the world. We don't want you to have an offensive military capability. We want you to have a self-defense force just as you are doing—modern ships, modern aircraft, surveillance gear—keep that up. But you've got to do something else. Security is much more than ships and tanks and airplanes. It's the economic growth of developing nations. Why don't you triple your economic aid to the Philippines? Give them economic aid, so that Aquino can put those economic goods and services up where the insurgency is and remove the threat to Subic Bay and Clark Field. They are thinking seriously about that, because the chairman of our economic committee is Paul Volcker and the chairman of our security committee is General Andrew J. Goodpaster. They both just came back from Tokyo, and we are going to put out a white paper in April addressing this very question about integrating security and economics into a way that will give us a better structure for peace around the world, and doing it while we're trying to stay strong enough to be stable in our draw down with the Soviet Union.

QUESTION: I'm concerned about the euphoria around the comments that are coming out of Russia now. Do you see in this or did you hear any indication of a change in the basic doctrine of world communism that the Russians put forth over the years? For instance, do the recent talks between the Russians and the Chinese have any foreboding sign for us?

GENERAL SEIGNIOUS: Yes, we did hear statements while we were in the Soviet Union and have read and studied statements made by Gorbachev since then. There is a lot less euphoria in the Soviet Union about internal progress than there was two years ago, because they are becoming much more realistic about the tremendous period of time it's going to take to reform the economic structure in the Soviet Union.

Yes, there is much too much euphoria in Western Europe, particularly in Germany. It's causing some great concerns in the alliance and certainly in the United States that Genscher, the foreign minister, is moving out much too euphorically and much too aggressively for all kinds of changes in the vision of cohesion for the alliance, his gestures toward including a nuclear-free zone, excessive credits to Eastern European countries, and a petition for a change in our technology standards so that computers and that kind of thing can be sent to Eastern Europe, including the Soviet Union. There is much too much euphoria.

I've raised this with Egon Bahr, who is the so-called political philosopher for the SDP (Social Democratic party of the Federal Republic of Germany). He said, "Well, we think we are right in being more forward and more optimistic than the United States, because we think that this is real. We think we can afford to move somewhat faster than you in the West who are still much more skeptical than we are agreed to." That's my point, that the Soviet Union says that Eastern European countries are free to develop their own social and political systems for their own by themselves; but they have not explicitly renounced the Brezhnev Doctrine, for example. They say that the Soviet Union cannot achieve its goals by the use of military force, but they are still supporting Castro in Cuba. They say that the basic doctrine of communism calling for a struggle of the working class is no longer a part of their doctrine. In a rhetorical sense they have pulled the teeth from many of the things that have been historically thought of as ironclad laws of communism. They are disclaiming a lot of that, but the progress of those deeds that correspond to those declaratory policies have not yet built up a level of confidence so that we can begin to alter our strategies and our doctrines.

QUESTION: We really didn't need Gorbachev to tell us how badly the Soviets were doing, certainly for the past two decades. People in the embassy have been sending back reports; I can vouch for that. I spent five years during which five months out of each year I traveled. Back in 1964, 47 percent of all their machine tool equipment resources were spent on repairs. Their quality control was zilch. Their crawler tractors are the basis of their tanks; only 13 hours off the assembly line some break down, needing major repairs. All these things we've known for decades. My question is why our policy was always oriented toward the sort of super military strength which I think would not have been as super if we had challenged it because they didn't have the power to sustain it. Our administrations knew all this. Our policy was not oriented toward these weaknesses. Instead we had this grand business where leaders met leaders. For example, I sat in on a very intimate dinner at the ambassador's residence with Harriman during the Berlin crises. Khrushchev sat on the other side; Mikoyan, Kosygin, and the whole crew were there. After the dinner, the cigars and the cognac came out, and Khrushchev gets up and says, "Permit me to tell an anti-Soviet joke." So the top people were in communication, but nothing really resulted out of that. Harriman says, "Mr. Prime Minister, I like the *dacha* I'm in. If you give me a *dacha*, I'll come and be your adviser." Khrushchev laughs a little and says, "It's yours. But I don't have to take your advice."

We knew all about these social and economic problems. Why were we so timid about everything? For example, Hungary, Czechoslovakia—we did nothing about these things, but we knew the weaknesses. That's my question.

GENERAL SEIGNIOUS: That's a hell of a question. I've got to answer with one vignette of my own. I was at the signing of SALT II, and Brezhnev had a dinner for President Carter. On one side of the table sat Brezhnev and the leaders, on the other side was Mr. Carter, and the Soviets were interspersed.

Brezhnev raised his glass of white wine and toasted the President of the United States and the United States of America and drained the glass, and then as a Soviet custom he held the glass right over his head and not a drop of wine spilled. You know what happened. Our "born-again" President, who didn't know much about white wine, raised his glass, toasted Mr. Brezhnev very properly, but he forgot to empty it, and when he held the glass over his head, you know what happened—it spilled everywhere.

To answer that serious question, I would tell you I think the risk of nuclear war is the answer. We would not have responded in a regional crisis to prevent or in any way to cause a withdrawal of Soviet forces from Hungary when they were in possession of nuclear weapons. We came close enough in Cuba in 1962. The Cuban missile crisis, if you read the history of it, is a pretty spooky event. We won, but we went to the brink of nuclear war. As a soldier, I tell you I hesitate to go to that brink, because I don't know what we achieve by doing it. I don't think we could have exploited the economic and social weaknesses in Soviet structure. I think we would have put at risk our civilization and our economic and social structure, and you have to measure those risks very carefully.

QUESTION: Did you happen to read McGeorge Bundy's review of John Mueller's doomsday book in yesterday's paper?

GENERAL SEIGNIOUS: No, I did not.

COMMENT: The thesis is that really what has stopped us and the Russians is not what Churchill called "the balance of terror," but rather the fear of conventional war, which has become so terrible that it is now a deterrent in itself. Bundy more or less agrees with this University of Rochester professor.

GENERAL SEIGNIOUS: I do not agree with McGeorge Bundy's postulation of conventional forces as being adequate for deterrence on the Western European scene. This has been tried for a thousand years, and people always misjudge what one conventional force can do to the other; I think for many years to come the nuclear component of our deterrence is an essential component. McGeorge Bundy signed that "no first use" proposition, and I don't subscribe to that. I think it would lessen our deterrent.

QUESTION: Aren't we going to have a severe dilemma when they have elections in Germany? The coalition between the CDU, the CSU, and the democratic opposition could be affected by Genscher's "new thinking."

GENERAL SEIGNIOUS: I think there is a great risk if we in the West are not sensitive to the political content of our relationship with Germany; if we are insensitive, we will run a high risk of a loss of cohesion in the alliance. I'm neither an SDPer or a CDUer in political terms, and I try to stay fairly bipartisan here in this country. But I'll tell you, if we press Kohl to the point of making a decision in the next 90 days on the modernization of the Lance system, I think it will run the risk of Kohl's losing political clout in his country and enhance the possibility of the SDP being elected. The SDP has not been supportive of Western strategy, which threatens cohesion in the alliance. They've come up with some harebrained notions that are as bad as the Labour party's ideas in Great Britain, and I would think it would be a disaster for the West if the left wing of the SDP were to be elected. If we had a Schmidt, who is to the center, that would be less risky. But the current leadership of the SDP is highly risky as far as defense policy and NATO unity is concerned. We could aid and abet the success of the left coming in if we take extraordinary steps to put Kohl in a box that he can't get out of in a domestic political sense. I think it would be a big error.

QUESTION: How do the Soviet Union's aging, entrenched bureaucracy and military fit into Gorbachev's situation?

GENERAL SEIGNIOUS: Let me give you one indicator that I didn't bring out in my comments. In late September when we were there, General Batalin from the Central Committee met with us and presented a very learned document with great clarity and high intelligence. He said, "One thing that you gentlemen from the United States should understand is that we in the military think that it's nonsense to engage in unilateral military moves without compensating acts on your part, and therefore the Soviet Union will not engage in unilateral acts of withdrawal." The significance of what I am saying to you is that on 7 December 1988 in New York, Gorbachev apparently overrode all of his military and made the decision to announce rather spectacular unilateral acts of withdrawal.

The military is to be reckoned with certainly, and you'll hear from it as this new five-year plan unfolds in 1991. Maybe they will want so much in their so called "reasonable sufficiency" that it will appear unreasonable to us. I don't know how it will ever come out, but I do think that it's safe to say that Gorbachev had not really tackled his military until he made the decision on this unilateral withdrawal. Of course, the chief of the general staff resigned within 12 hours of the time he made that declaration.

QUESTION: Life was so much simpler, as you recall, in the "tough" cold war days when you knew what to do. I'm reminded of a situation in which we have not only 16 cooks on our side, but all the cooks on their side as well trying to make this new "tapestry." I mixed my metaphors, but it's appropriate on this occasion because everything is so mixed up. The fact is that the steps we now take in response to the Soviet moves seem crucial. Isn't one of the first steps that can be taken a withdrawal to the point where there is not a direct confrontation and the reduction of forces to the point where both sides have confidence that there is time?

GENERAL SEIGNIOUS: That's very sensible, in spite of "cooked tapestry." I think the import of what you are saying is that West-West relations in the coming months and years are equally as critical as East-West relations, because if we don't have this vision of how we move together, you can be sure that our movements separately will be to the disadvantage of the West.

I do think there is some credibility in the negotiating posture for zones that deny offensive weapons to be in those zones—tanks, artillery, bridging equipment, and armored personnel carriers. If we could find a structure asymmetrical because of the differences in the terrain, the Soviet Union would draw back, say, 100 kilometers and have a zone that was absolutely verifiable with no real offensive equipment. It would have stability and each side would have substantial warning time. If we reach the point where we've got 120 days or more of time to react to substantial evidence occurring on the ground, and have the political will and wisdom, we can do a lot to redress any imbalance. What we don't have now is the ability to redress the imbalance in time, because they've got the capability for surprise invasion. That's what we are negotiating about, to remove that first. I think step by step, if we do it prudently and cohesively, we will have a structure that will give us adequate timing.

QUESTION: Do we ever dare address Soviet involvement in Cuba and Cuban involvement in Africa in negotiating with Russia in their new sort of approach to things?

GENERAL SEIGNIOUS: Yes, there is no question about the fact that we are not engaged in a one-track policy with the Soviet Union. We are engaged in at least a two-track one, and Soviet behavior internationally is one of those tracks. We should raise it in spades, and I think we have begun to do so.

I think it was begun under Mr. Reagan officially, and I know personally it was done at our level, although we are nongovernmental. We did raise these issues, that if you want credibility with us in the West you've got to behave internationally in a civilized way. The support of surrogate forces around the world is not civilized behavior.

NARRATOR: What we have heard is a very significant and memorable blending of strength, diplomacy, and prudence. Churchill said on some 70 occasions after the Fulton speech that we have to look for openings, and we do have to think about opportunities. It seems fortunate that we have the kind of soldier-statesmen who are constantly thinking about this, and that they happen to be in very strategic locations.

CHAPTER 9

Jean Monnet—The Man and The Vision

AMBASSADOR JOHN W. TUTHILL

As the European Community regains momentum to approach the goal of a free internal market (of persons, merchandise, services, and capital) of over 320 million people by 1992, there is an increased interest in the work, objectives, and perseverance of the man more responsible than any other for the post-World War II movement towards a united Europe. Most of the analysis has been of how this man—Jean Monnet—managed to reason, cajole, argue, circumvent, and bully the reluctant European governments towards a sharing or pooling of national sovereignty. But the analysts have, for the most part, lost sight of the man from the Cognac area who never lost the strength, shrewdness, superstitions, and realistic self-appraisal of that basic strength of France—the men of the soil.[1]

Much has been written about Monnet. He has been—quite correctly—called "The Architect and Master Builder of the European Economic Community." A perceptive description of Monnet's ideals and objectives can be found in George Ball's brief and moving introduction to Monnet's "Memoirs."[2] The emphasis on Monnet's goals and methods of achieving

189

them tend, however, to obscure the man. From the time of my assignment at the American Embassy in Paris in 1956 until Monnet's death two decades later, I had the unusual opportunity and great good fortune to be with him often, both officially and personally.

George Ball shared Monnet's determination to struggle for European unity. Ball and a number of other Americans were convinced that the individual countries in Europe, standing alone and with each carefully guarding its sovereignty, did not represent viable long-term partners for the United States. Technological developments and the aftermath of the war left the individual European states inherently too weak in geopolitical, economic, and military terms. America needed and still needs stronger and united democratic allies. Most U.S. governments in the first decades after World War II supported Monnet's vision of a truly united Europe. Amongst those who shared his views were most U.S. presidents, and particularly Franklin D. Roosevelt, Dwight D. Eisenhower, John F. Kennedy, and Lyndon B. Johnson, as well as secretaries of state Dulles, Herter, and Rusk and any number of influential officials and private individuals, including John J. McCloy, David Bruce, Douglas Dillon, and George Ball. There were, in fact, times when it was not an exaggeration to say that the American government was more "for European unity" than the Europeans. Certainly it was, from time to time, correct to say this regarding certain individual European governments.

Now that the centenary celebration of Monnet's birth (1988) has come and gone and after the plaque has been unveiled at the office he occupied from 1956-76 at 83 Avenue Foch, Paris, and his ashes have been moved—in an impressive ceremony—to the Pantheon, the resting place of many famous Frenchmen, the time has come to shed more light on the personal attributes, the inner strengths, the acknowledged limitations, and the seductive powers of this man who has perhaps done more than any one person to shape the world of the Atlantic nations in the second half of the 20th century.

At a meeting of the American Enterprise Institute in Washington, D.C., in early 1988, Otto von Hapsburg (now a resident of Bavaria and a member of the Christian Socialist Union) spoke in glowing terms of Charles de Gaulle, citing de Gaulle's alleged key role in building European unity. Hapsburg, in his innocence or deviousness, referred to the Adenauer-de Gaulle agreement in January 1963 as a milestone towards a united Europe.

In fact, de Gaulle, a most articulate advocate of the nation-state, was publicly and proudly opposed to the sharing of sovereignty which was, and is, essential for a united Europe. The historic meeting and agreement of de Gaulle and Adenauer in January 1963 came only shortly after de Gaulle had vetoed British entry into the European Community charging, amongst other things, that Britain would be the "wooden horse" of American interests.

There was a real attraction between Adenauer and de Gaulle. Each had something approaching disdain for his own compatriots. De Gaulle is alleged to have stated, "The French will only be united under the threat of danger. Nobody can simply bring together a country that has 265 different kinds of cheese." Adenauer had vigorously supported Jean Monnet in the movement towards European unity. When de Gaulle separated France from the other five Common Market countries in vetoing British membership, Adenauer must have been torn between his support for European unity and his conviction of the need for French-German reconciliation.

When de Gaulle and Adenauer announced their January 1963 bilateral agreement, there was deep worry amongst knowledgeable persons in Europe and in the United States who favored a truly united Europe based upon strong institutions. Few dared, however, to voice this concern directly and personally to the two leaders. One of those who did was Walter Hallstein, then president of the European Commission. I was told, at the time, that Adenauer was "furious" at Hallstein (who had been in charge of the German Foreign Office before becoming president of the commission) because Hallstein advised him personally that instead of creating Europe, the bilateral French-German agreement threatened its very existence.

Monnet always had in mind a European institutional structure which would provide the framework within which Germany and France would work together and which would firmly anchor Western Germany with the Western democratic world. Monnet felt the two aging leaders, while properly motivated in terms of the need for German-French reconciliation, were wrong in attempting to achieve it via bilateral agreements.

In his memoirs Monnet described his concern regarding the bilateral treaty when various views were being publicized. He wrote, "Meanwhile, we had written a gloss on the Franco-German Treaty, which the parliamentary strategists turned into a preamble."[3] He managed to turn an obstacle into a step forward. Subsequently, the German Bundestag inserted a preamble to the agreement which provided "the maintenance and strengthening of the cohesion of free peoples, and in particular close cooperation between the United States and Europe, common defense within NATO, and the union of Europe, including the United Kingdom,"[4] thus placing the agreement within an appropriate context.

Monnet, in facing problems, used to say, "Let us not sit on opposite sides of the table with the problem between us. Let us sit on the same side of the table and put the problem on the other side and solve it." He used to carry in his wallet a quotation from Ibn Saud, "For me, everything is a means— even the obstacles." Monnet's skillful treatment of a disturbing bilateral agreement by managing to have it placed within the context of a united Europe and an Atlantic alliance involving the United States took a problem and, together with his friends in Europe, converted it into the means for progress.

Those of us who had been alarmed by the apparent narrow, bilateral nature of the Adenauer-de Gaulle agreement may have underestimated the underlying strength of the urge towards European unity and the absolute need for French-German agreement within an institutional structure. To quote T. S. Eliot, "We had the experience but did not understand the meaning." In any event, thanks to the Monnet-inspired preamble, developments since 1963 have channeled that initially bilateral agreement along lines that are not only constructive but essential for true European unity. Two of the European leaders who played a vital role in this evolution were Valéry Giscard d'Estaing and Helmut Schmidt, who achieved specific progress in dealing with European problems such as a European monetary system (still in 1988 without Britain) and regular meetings of heads of governments and the direct elections of a European parliament. They strengthened an institutional structure within which German-French collaboration was essential for continuing progress toward European unity.

Monnet was convinced that only by overriding the entrenched bureaucracies in European national governments could unification be achieved. He knew that many bureaucrats in high places would be skeptical or would vigorously oppose moves towards European unity which involved sharing of some of their national powers. Based upon his influence with the heads of governments and his conviction that the ideas furthering unity were right, he was prepared to wait them out. To Monnet, "sovereignty" was the continuing villain. De Gaulle, on the other hand, in the 1960s was the prime supporter of "sovereignty." But national views can change. *The Economist*[5] has noted the French in 1988 "broadly accept that sovereignty, unlike virginity, can be lost in stages and . . . can also be shared."

Monnet would have been embarrassed by the question of credit for uniting Europe. He wanted institutions involving commitments which would survive. He wrote, "When an idea answers to the needs of an epoch, it ceases to belong to those who invented it and becomes more powerful than those who serve it."[6]

In December 1960, after the election of Kennedy and Johnson, the vice-presidential designate and Senator William Fulbright visited Paris. I was in Paris at that time negotiating the new organization which became the Organization for Economic Cooperation and Development (OECD). At George Ball's request I made an appointment for Johnson and Fulbright to meet Monnet. During the drive from the hotel to Monnet's office Johnson took out a letter which he read to Fulbright and me which clearly came from a close friend who wrote, "What's a Texas cowboy like you doing meeting with a French philosopher like Monnet?" Subsequently I learned that that letter was from Phil Graham of the *Washington Post*.

To the extent that I could be heard through the rush of words from Johnson, I pointed out that the author of the letter did not understand Monnet. I stated that Monnet, without a university education, came from the soil of the Cognac region in France (he started life peddling that splendid product, Monnet Cognac). Monnet had all of the strength and shrewdness of a French peasant, which he combined with an extraordinary personal knowledge of many key people throughout the world. He would have ridiculed the description of himself as a "philosopher."

Monnet's single-minded drive for European unity can be illustrated by his treatment of the revolving door of American ambassadors who wandered in and out of Paris during the postwar years. He had one message for each American ambassador—most of whom failed to understand or act upon it. The message was this: The Europeans were creating a unified Europe of equal partners. Monnet hoped that the American ambassador in Paris would be successful in encouraging strong French-American relations, but he urged America not to make any agreement with France that it was not prepared to offer to Germany.

When I was ambassador to the OECD in 1961, President Kennedy sent General Gavin to France as American ambassador on the naive assumption that a general could deal effectively—as equals—with de Gaulle. This might have been appropriate for generals Eisenhower and Marshall, but other American generals had little more status with de Gaulle than junior officers. Monnet asked me if I could arrange a meeting with Gavin, which I did at a luncheon in my home at Neuilly with just the three of us present. The luncheon, while pleasant, was a disaster in terms of getting the message across. General Gavin was so impressed by the U.S. space program and its offshoots that he insisted that Monnet should listen to the ticking of his watch, which in some way reflected side benefits of the U.S. space program. As for Monnet's main theme, I saw no indication that Gavin understood or reacted one way or another.

It should be added that Monnet's policy of non-discrimination, especially in terms of Germany, included nuclear agreements. That was the basis of Monnet's support for Professor Bowie's proposal of a European Multilateral Nuclear Force. Monnet felt that Germany should have an important role in all aspects of security, including nuclear. After Lyndon Johnson withdrew American support in the 1960s for this proposal, it was clear that the time had not yet arrived for Europe and America to deal with this difficult subject.

Monnet's emphasis upon clear objectives lead him to resist interference of events or people not consistent with the attainment of those objectives. He did not see any reason to spend time (or waste time, in his view) with people not involved in the pursuit of such objectives. Accordingly, he was not interested in "small talk" on unrelated subjects. This characteristic can be illustrated by a dinner given by the American ambassador to France.

In 1961 and 1962 I was fully occupied with the early stages in getting the OECD going. One day Monnet showed me an invitation to a black tie dinner by the then American ambassador to France, Amory Houghton. He looked at me and said, "What shall I do with this?" I said, "You can either accept it or regret it." My response annoyed him. He demanded to know why he should accept and asked me who would be at the dinner. I assured him that I had no idea whatsoever and told him I was no longer part of the American Embassy to France and that the Houghton dinner was outside of my interest or control. Monnet felt I was not being helpful.

Subsequently I saw Monnet after the dinner, which he had attended. He was furious—with me. He stated, "You should have warned me." He stated that after cocktails everyone proceeded to the dinner table, where he was seated between Madame Couve de Murville and the socially conscious wife of a senior American Embassy official. He said that he had known Madame de Murville for 20 to 30 years and had exhausted all subjects of conversation with her. As to the wife of the American Embassy official, he demanded, "What was I supposed to talk about with her?" In fact, the Embassy wife is a very intelligent and well-informed person, but not on the subject of European unity. She was of no interest to Monnet.

The Duke and Duchess of Windsor were the guests of honor. After dinner the men retired for coffee and cognac. Monnet stated that he expected, at least in that male group, there would be some serious conversation. On the contrary, as soon as the cognac had been consumed the ambassador announced, "Shall we join the ladies?" Monnet was escorted into the next room and seated next to the Duchess of Windsor. He always felt that I was to blame for that—to him—disastrous evening.

From the early days when the Coal and Steel Community was formed, Monnet supported, argued, and fought for Britain as a part of the European unity movement. This effort was intensified once the Common Market was in place. In the early 1960s I mentioned to him that if Britain came in, Norway and Denmark would also have to be invited. He was appalled by that thought. He demanded to know why, and despite my explanation, he remained adamantly opposed to Scandinavian membership. Subsequently, of course, Norway was invited and then, in a referendum, decided not to join; Denmark remains today a member. I can well imagine what Monnet's reaction would be regarding Portuguese, Spanish, Greek, and the prospect of Turkish membership, to say nothing of the possibility of adding the neutrals—Austria, Sweden, and Switzerland. If you will, Monnet wanted a "little Europe" consisting of those major democratic countries whose economic and political structures were sufficiently harmonious to allow them to seek agreement on basic policies.

Have events overtaken Monnet's emphasis upon the major European powers? Can a community of 12—and perhaps in the future 16, 17, or 18—function? Surely not in the sense of the original six and the expectation that, sooner or later, Britain would join. But there may be future developments which will create and reinforce a nucleus within the enlarged community. In order to create the inner harmony on economic and political policies—and in the future, military and security issues as well—conditions must exist within nations of basically compatible political and social structures. This may still be achieved—possibly with the assistance of the long-neglected Western European union—in order that the key nations may move forward together without slowing their progress to the slower ships in the convoy.[7]

Monnet favored an Atlantic alliance based upon North America (he would include Canada, but without much enthusiasm) and a unified Europe. He supported the general objectives of the OECD based upon the hope (unfulfilled) that within that organization the six—and later to include the British—would act as a unit. Again his views about the Scandinavians in the European Community and the smaller countries' minor role within the OECD reflected his emphasis upon the key sources of political power. Lesser nations were of little interest to him.

Monnet resisted distractions. The most acrimonious meeting I ever had with him and George Ball was at a luncheon at my home in Neuilly during the early days of the Kennedy administration. Ball stated that the view in "The White House" was that the allies were on a "collision course" in Berlin and that something should be done about it.

Monnet, who at that time had very little interest in Berlin, joined Ball in wishing to seek ways in which the American, British, and French role in Berlin could be altered, reduced, or eliminated. I had been in Berlin from late June 1945, at the time of the Potsdam Conference, and had continued off and on until the summer of 1947. I was again in Germany and Berlin in the American Embassy from 1952 to 1956. I had then, and still have, strong views about the position of the Western powers in Berlin. I gave Monnet and Ball a heated presentation saying that nations, like individuals, inherit certain obligations which cannot be avoided without loss of integrity. I stated that the Berlin obligation was one of those and that, in my view, there was no way for the allies basically to alter their obligations. We had to stand firm.

Several months after that conversation President Kennedy made his first trip to Europe as president. By this time Kennedy and perhaps the rest of the new administration had become reconciled to the existence of our responsibilities in Berlin. This visit to Berlin was the occasion for Kennedy to issue his well-known and thrilling words about Berlin being a fortress of democracy surrounded by a communist world and to proclaim, "Ich bin ein Berliner."

There were other sides to Monnet. For example, one weekend I was out at his home at Houjarray outside of Paris for a Sunday dinner with his wife Sylvia, his daughter Marianne, and himself. His wife served chicken with a carafe of white wine. Monnet tasted the wine, made a face, and demanded, "What is this?" His wife said that this was a white wine that the village people recommended very highly. Monnet replied, "I don't like it." Then Sylvia turned to me and said, "Several years ago David Bruce was here for dinner. We served a muscadet which David enjoyed. Since then Jean insists that we serve only that wine." Monnet sheepishly turned to me and to his wife and said, "And why not? David Bruce knows more about French wines than I'll ever know." I think this an unusual example of a Frenchman insisting on a wine recommended by an American.

Monnet's attachment to America was reflected in his annual celebration of thanksgiving—American style. For years my contribution to this sentimental dinner was to purchase and present to him a U.S. Embassy commissary frozen turkey, together with the necessary cranberry sauce and other fixings. After I left Paris I turned over that happy responsibility to a colleague. I believe Monnet maintained this tradition to the end.

Monnet carried with him many of the superstitions of the French peasants. During the Kennedy administration George Ball visited Europe frequently. After each visit he and Monnet and I would have breakfast at the Plaza Athene, after which Ball would take off for the airport. After one such visit, Monnet and I were walking down Avenue Montaigne waving farewell to Ball, when Monnet stepped in a rather large dog muss. He turned to me and said, "Oh, it's all right. It's good luck." For once I remembered more about one French superstition than Monnet, and I replied, "It's only good luck, Jean, if you step into it with your left foot." Monnet said, "That's right," and immediately took his left foot and placed it firmly in the dog muss.

It is also accurate to say that—in the right sense and for real purposes—Monnet "used" people. His contacts with many undoubtedly reflected that. From 1956 until 1966, I was successively minister for economic affairs at the American Embassy, Paris; American ambassador to the OECD; and U.S. representative to the European Community. Therefore, Monnet was interested in me. I noted the same tendency with many others. He exploited, in the proper sense of the word, the expertise of people competent in special fields, be it nuclear, monetary, industrial cartels, institutions, etc. Once he had exhausted the particular subject and the individual, he tended to lose interest in the person giving him the advice.

Monnet's sense of the loci of political power did not hinder him from identifying and working closely with individuals of talent and knowledge of subjects in some way related to European unity. Many such individuals were very young and came from government bureaucracies, the media, and academe. In my case, once I was named ambassador to Brazil in 1966, we almost lost touch—at least until I returned to Paris three years later as head of a research organization concerned with Atlantic and European affairs. While Monnet sought people who could help him in achieving his objectives, he did not go as far as Robert Campos in Brazil, who maintained that, "Men should consort with men with a future and women with a past."

In his address of 13 September 1988 before the Council on Foreign Relations, George Ball noted an important secret to Monnet's effectiveness, i.e., "his lack of personal ambition." As Ball pointed out, "Because he never challenged a political figure as a rival, he could easily gain his audience." This point has not been sufficiently emphasized. Many—or perhaps most—advocates of strong positions in government policies are suspect because of the sometimes all too obvious personal political advantage that they wish to achieve via their advocacy.

An illustration of Monnet's emphasis on action—and, if necessary, battle—is to be found in his comments on the Development Assistance Committee (then known as the Development Assistance Group—DAG) which became part of the OECD in early 1961. The Development Assistance Committee (DAC) was formed in order to achieve "an increased and improved flow of aid to the developing countries." The word *improved* referred to the conviction that more of the assistance should be either in grants or very long-term and low (subsidized) interest loans. The DAC with OECD members and Japan (Japan was not yet an OECD member) was designed to exert pressure on each of the affluent industrialized countries to do more for the developing world.

When the DAC was formed, a distinguished but rather orthodox American ambassador was named as the first chairman. After the committee had been in existence for several months, Monnet asked me how things were going in that committee. I replied in a bland sort of way that all was going well. Monnet said, "Are there any disputes and serious arguments?" I replied, "No, not really." Monnet looked at me disdainfully and said, "If there are no disputes and arguments, there is also no progress." He was right; the DAC at that stage was stagnant.

Monnet had an unfailing sense of the sources of political power. His Action Committee for the United States of Europe consisted of the top representatives of (1) the conservative parties of Europe, (2) the socialist parties, and (3) the key noncommunist European trade unions. He often said to me that he did not worry about governments; if he had support from the two major parties, country by country, and the trade unions, the government bureaucrats couldn't stop a proposal. Monnet always stressed the word *action* in the title of his commission. He was not interested in running a think tank. He wanted specific proposals that would help propel Europe towards unity.

At the start of the European Community, and especially with the European Commission in Brussels during the time when I was the American ambassador accredited to the commission and Euratom (European Atomic Energy Commission), the commission and Euratom were staffed by bureaucrats from the six governments. In 28 years in the United States government I never worked with a bureaucracy as creative, motivated, and persevering as the personnel in the European Commission, which then was headed by Walter Hallstein as president, with vice presidents Robert Marjolin and Sicco Mansholt and with Jean Rey, in effect, as foreign minister. The commissioners and their staffs were all basically in Brussels because they wanted to contribute to the creation of something that they—and I—felt essential, namely a united Europe which would rise above the national objectives of the six participating countries. The same was true of the Euratom commissioners and staff. These officials qualified for the second category of people who, according to Monnet, wanted to "do something" rather than to "be somebody."

Between the two world wars Monnet went to China as adviser to that government on the construction of the railway system. He and his staff became frustrated in efforts to understand precisely what the Chinese wanted. Monnet told me that he called his staff together and said, "I don't think we'll ever fully understand the Chinese. Therefore it is essential that they understand us."

Monnet had his first experience working with an international institution when, after World War I, he became deputy secretary of the League of Nations. He held that position for approximately five years, from 1919 until 1924. This experience with an institution with no basic executive authority and incomplete membership (i.e., the absence of the United States of America) must have conditioned Monnet towards building institutions not unduly fettered by national governments. In brief, Monnet dreamed of a united Europe which could deal as an equal with the United States and thus create a permanent Atlantic alliance consisting of the two democratic pillars, one in Europe and one in North America.

Members of the American Foreign Service generally were not fully aware of and therefore gave insufficient consideration to the role of labor in foreign policy. One of the outstanding persons in helping to nudge United States foreign policy after World War II into a realization of Stalin's objectives was the AFL-CIO man in Berlin, Irving Brown. It was through Brown that I had the opportunity to know George Meany, then president of the AFL-CIO. I dare say that there were not many ambassadorial offices throughout the world in which there was a framed, autographed picture of the president of the AFL-CIO, but there was one in mine.

On the occasion of one of his trips to Europe, I asked Meany if he would like to meet Monnet. He agreed immediately. From that time on, every time Meany visited Europe (and it was fairly often) I arranged a luncheon in my home just for Meany and Monnet. This Frenchman from the Cognac area and the American labor leader got along like a house afire. They both insisted upon coming directly to grips with the essence of each subject under discussion, and they were almost always in agreement. At one time when I saw Meany in Washington he mentioned a prominent American who was about to visit Europe and said to me, "Will he see Monnet?" I replied, "As far as I know, he will not." Meany grumbled, "That's unfortunate. I am just a plumber, but I wouldn't think of going to Europe without seeing Monnet."

Monnet was convinced that there are "lucky" and "unlucky" people. He was not an admirer of Ludwig Erhard, who succeeded Konrad Adenauer as German chancellor. There was at that time much praise for Erhard's currency and economic reforms, which had supported Germany's economic recovery. In discussing Erhard, I pointed out that the timing had been propitious for the financial and economic reforms which he had put into effect in Germany. He had been "lucky." Monnet exclaimed, "Don't tell me he is lucky."

Monnet was against recording machines. On the other hand, he spent hours on the telephone with key officials in Bonn, Brussels, London, and elsewhere. One time when I was with him, he received an international call and conversed at some length regarding a sensitive issue under negotiation. De Gaulle was president of France. Monnet was advocating policies in direct conflict with de Gaulle's objectives. When he finished, I asked if it would be prudent to assume that his phone was tapped (it surely was) and to be careful in such conversations. He waved aside my advice saying, "Yes, I know. Let them listen. If they learn something, it'll be to the good."

The last time I saw Monnet, several months before his death and when the European movement was in the doldrums, I found him depressed about both his health and the then stagnation of the European Community. After a rambling conversation, he said, "Well, if nothing else, we have created a framework which eliminates the possibility of another Franco-German war." I replied, "My dear friend, that alone represents one of the major contributions of this century."

ENDNOTES

1. One of his collaborators, Jacques Van Helmont, in an excellent essay entitled "Jean Monnet—comme il était," has described working with this man who never attended a university nor was elected to public office. Published by Foundation Jean Monnet pour l'Europe, Centre de Recherches Européennes, Lausanne, 1981.

2. Jean Monnet, "Memoirs" (New York: Doubleday, 1978), pp. 11-14 (translation by Richard Mayne).

3. Ibid., p. 468.

4. Ibid., p. 468.

5. Issue of 5 November 1988, p. 51.

6. Jean Monnet, "Memoirs," p. 510.

7. See René Foch, *L'Europe en construction*, Centre Inter-professionnel de Promotion Économique et Sociale Nord Franche-Comte, pages 22-23, for a presentation of these possibilities including quotations from Jacques Delors, president of the European Commission concerning possible future membership or close collaboration not only of the European neutrals but also East Germany, Hungary, and Czechoslovakia.

IV.

THE RHETORIC
OF DISCOURSE
AMONG STATESMEN

CHAPTER 10

Presidential Rhetoric and Political Discourse

LADD HAMILTON

NARRATOR: From Alexis de Tocqueville to the present, almost every observer of the American scene has talked about the size and expanse and diversity of the country. Tocqueville called attention to different cultural patterns, as well as to the unique talents that people in various regions, sections, and cities contributed to the national dialogue. The only problem is that we tend to be insular, and Tocqueville observed that, too. We know the New Englanders, if we are New Englanders; we know the New Yorkers, if we are New Yorkers. Sometimes we know mainly the Virginians, if we are Virginians. So today is a banner day at the Miller Center; it is a banner day for our guests because yesterday was their wedding anniversary. It is an anniversary of sorts for us in that we have an opportunity to hear a respected regional journalist from another part of the country, well known in that region but not so well known in our Virginia.

Ladd Hamilton wrote a column that inspired attention and discussion in the *New York Times*. He made the radical suggestion that one reason we don't know our presidential candidates is that they don't give us their own thoughts. Their thoughts are filtered through the minds and words of wordsmiths who coin their phrases and tell them and the public what the candidate thinks. That is a different view from that of most contemporary speech writers.

Ladd Hamilton was born in Los Angeles but lived most of his life in Idaho. He studied at the University of Idaho; he began writing for a daily newspaper in Oregon, but then returned to Lewiston, Idaho, where he spent the remainder of his active journalist career. He began as a reporter for the *Morning Tribune*; he worked his way up covering all the desks in that paper, becoming managing editor in 1972 and senior editor in 1977. In that capacity as senior editor he mainly wrote editorials and columns for the paper, and some of these were picked up in other parts of the country. He retired last year as senior editor and has been doing some free-lance writing. He has a forthcoming book that all of us look forward to seeing.

MR. HAMILTON: Thank you, Mr. Thompson. I would like to take us all back to a moment in an earlier presidential campaign. Hubert Humphrey is finishing an address. He picks up the text, puts it in his pocket and says, "And now for a few words of my own." His audience is mildly amused at his candor, but nobody is startled, much less shocked, on learning that the candidate has delivered somebody else's speech.

And no wonder. It has been a long time and many administrations since presidents and political candidates have written their own speeches. Members of the general public may still believe—or pretend because they *want* to believe—that their leaders speak to them in their own words. But most know better, and no one knows this better than the members of the press. These people assume—being either realists or cynics—that practically everything said by presidents and candidates is written out for them by somebody else. Even some members of the press—among them some of the most prominent people who are writing opinion pieces for the press—do not write all their own columns. Many are written by researchers or legmen under the bylines of their bosses. So there is a great deal of ambivalence, if not outright hypocrisy, in the way the press sometimes condemns political ghostwriting while contributing to it.

Last April 17, on the op-ed page of the *New York Times*, James Reston, a *Times* senior editor, complained about the practice of passing off as one's own the words of another. I quote:

> The result is that we know the Great Men who read the statements, often over teleprompters, which give the impression that they just thought them all up. But the people who wrote them and drafted the policies are usually unelected, unconfirmed, and mostly unavailable. ... A senator can read a speech from a Capitol Hill TV studio and whisk it by satellite to the voters in the state. One week it may be a speech by his expert on the farm problems of the Middle West and the next on the tangles of the Middle East. This conveys the notion that the senator is a certified genius on almost everything and helps explain why 90 percent of the incumbents are reelected. ... None of this, unfortunately, seems to distress the public or even the press as much as it should.

Speaking as a former member of the press, I think it should, too. But Reston's own newspaper doesn't seem concerned. The deputy editor of the *Times* op-ed page, Kyle Crichton, told reporter Ari Posner recently that the editors of that page have "never rejected something because it was written by a ghostwriter." He told Posner, "If we insisted that every politician write his own piece, we'd either get terrible pieces or no pieces at all."

The editors of the *Times* op-ed page have made a Faustian bargain here. In return for better pieces, and lots of them, they have agreed to go along with the pretense that these politicians are writing their own stuff and therefore must know what they are talking about. The practice is fraudulent, and the *Times* is not the only culprit. David Broder, the chief political columnist of the *Washington Post*, asked in a recent column why our leaders should not be required to speak for themselves. Referring to Larry Speakes' revelation that he had put words in President Reagan's mouth, Broder wrote, "Perhaps the Speakes case will force us back to first principles and impel us, even at this late date, to ask the fundamental question: Why do any of them need a spokesman, unless they are unwilling or incapable of speaking for themselves?"

Broder writes with insight and conviction. Yet his own newspaper seems willing enough to publish ghostwritten pieces by important politicians. The policy of the *New York Times* in this respect is probably more the rule than the exception among newspapers.

According to Broder, "It's time for the press and the public to say to presidents and presidential candidates: Speak for yourselves." But this is not likely to happen. The present system, by which the press and the politicians feed each other, is working too well for both. It almost ensures the reelection of incumbent officeholders and keeps the papers supplied with well-written pieces under celebrity bylines.

What comforts the press and the politicians, however, may not sit so well with the voters. How are they to judge the typical candidate when they go to the polls? An issues paper produced by a staff is not much help. Issues change. What the candidate would do today about Panama may not mean anything a year from now. What the voters need is some insight into the candidate's mind and character. The question is not "What does he think?"; it is "*How* does he think?"

We haven't much doubt how Lincoln thought. We have the evidence of it in his words, written and spoken in the days before speech writers. We see Lincoln's mind at work in his prose. His language is the language of a good intellect and a compassionate heart. We can feel that we know Lincoln because he expressed himself to us in words that were his own and in phrasing as distinctive as his fingerprints.

And then there's Joe Biden. Before he quit the race for the Democratic nomination, Senator Biden was going from place to place delivering a speech he had borrowed from a Labour candidate for Parliament. It was a fine speech, but it was Neil Kinnock's speech, not Biden's, and when it came out that Biden was plagiarizing Kinnock, Biden decided to devote his time to the Iran-contra hearings.

That decision may tell us more about the American public than about Biden. He evidently perceived that the public would not let him get away with this masquerade. If his perception was right, and I think it may have been, then the public *does* care whether a candidate speaks his mind or someone else's. Then why don't we say so? Why don't we demand that the image makers back off and that the president speak to us directly instead of through bureaucratic filters? And why don't we insist that the candidates do the same? Perhaps we assumed long ago that it would do no good. Perhaps we have bought the line that our leaders and would-be leaders really are too busy to draft their own speeches and other public statements. For whatever reason, we have an odd reluctance to complain about a practice that has the effect of hiding our leaders behind false fronts.

Remember Spiro Agnew? He got a reputation as something of a wordsmith because his speeches were rich in alliterative flourishes—phrases like "the nattering nabobs of negativism," which we all remember so well. But the language was a false front; Agnew's best speeches were the work of a White House speech writer, William Safire. They tell us something about Safire, perhaps, but nothing about Agnew. Too bad. Understanding Agnew might have saved the country and the Nixon administration a lot of trouble.

A New York lawyer, Charles Rembar, makes the point resoundingly in his book, *The Law of the Land*:

> Historians and journalists do not hesitate to attribute fine sentences to a president when it is doubtful that the president created them, even when it should be obvious that the man has insufficient intellect to be the author of the words he speaks. Here the consequence is distortion of the voter's understanding.

Rembar continues, and this is the important part, I think:

> Ideas apart, style itself is one index of a person's mind and character, not by any means infallible but certainly evidentiary. We can be misled when the words are not the speaker's own. Intellect, whatever its failures, is generally desirable in a leader, and the electorate should be cognizant of its presence or absence.
>
> It might do something for the quality of our government if the press, instead of reporting that the president in his speech said this or that, reported that he selected this or that from what was offered him to say. Better still, the Constitution should be amended to require that the president must write, unaided, at last sixty percent of each speech he makes. Then, perhaps, in time we might get presidents like Jefferson or Lincoln instead of what we have.

We can know a candidate by his words and by the way he arranges them in sentences. But they must be his words and his sentences. As voters, we ought to have the right to know whether they are his or not; and if they are not, then we ought to ask why he cannot speak for himself.

If I may pick someone else's brain for a moment, here is a passage from a book review by Jack Beatty in the *Atlantic* of March 1988. The book is about Mario Cuomo, and Beatty is discussing one of the bases of Cuomo's appeal.

> In increasing numbers, people don't vote, because they don't grasp the relevance of the issues to their lives, pickled as the issues are in the elite jargon of policy entrepreneurs, who are just as happy to have the people shut out, uncomprehending, and quiescent. To get more of the public back into the public realm, the issues have first to be translated into what Wordsworth called "the real language of men." They have to be reclaimed for sense by metaphor.

And he quotes Cuomo on the quality the New York governor most admires in Lincoln: "his language—the magnificent way he communicated profound truths with simple images, simple words."

In this paragraph, Beatty touches on the essential quality of leadership, which is the ability to reach people, and perhaps to move them, through a language that is both common and eloquent. The Romans understood the power of oratory. Certainly Jesse Jackson and the other black Baptist preachers understand it.

Indeed, Jackson is a stunning example of the power of oratory—of simple images and simple words. Here is a man who has never held a government office; who is black; who carries a title, Reverend, that puts many people off. Yet he came very close to winning the presidential nomination of the Democratic party. How can it be explained except by the force of his personal rhetoric?

And how could the man who wasn't there—Mario Cuomo—have so dominated this election season had it not been for the power of *his* language? People respond to those who speak "the real language of men," and when our leaders understand this, the quality of government will improve.

To a large degree, language defines the speaker. And if I may be forgiven a brief digression, I would like to cite a good example of that from my own corner of the country. The Indians of the West—and perhaps of the East as well–traditionally have demanded eloquence in their leaders and frequently have gotten it, even in defeat. We can still be moved by the surrender speech of Chief Joseph of the Nez Percés in the snows of northern Montana in the bleak October of 1877:

> Tell General Howard I know his heart. What he told me before, I have in my heart. I am tired of fighting. Our chiefs are killed. Looking Glass is dead. Toohoolhoolzolte is dead. The old men are all dead. It is the young men who say yes or no. He who led the young men is dead. It is cold and we have no blankets. The little children are freezing to death. My people, some of them, have run away to the hills, and have no blankets, no food; no one knows where they are–perhaps freezing to death. I want to have time to look for my children and see how many I can find. Maybe I shall find them among the dead. Hear me, my chiefs. I am tired; my heart is sick and sad. From where the sun now stands, I will fight no more forever.

Those words were not only Joseph's. They *were* Joseph. That speech was taken down on the spot by General Howard's adjutant and was widely published, and yet people continued to think of Joseph as the warrior chief and the brilliant military strategist of the Nez Percés. He was a man of much influence, but other chiefs took charge of the fighting. Joseph's task, a crucial one, was to care for the old, the women, and the children so that the Indians could keep moving on the long retreat and no one would be left behind. Joseph's speech of surrender was the speech of a care giver, not a warrior. I don't understand how white Americans of the late nineteenth century could have missed that. Some of us even today continue to think of Chief Joseph as the brilliant military strategist.

If we know Tom Jefferson better than we know Lyndon Johnson, even from this distance—and not only on this campus—it is because we have so much of Jefferson in his own words. Jefferson, Franklin, and the other Founders are close and dear to us to this day because we have some right to feel that we know them—as indeed we do, from public utterances written by themselves.

I am going to close by suggesting that communication through hired hands may be cheating not only the voters but the candidates themselves. An end to this plague of ghostwriters would serve not only to enlighten the voters; it would also force the politicians to examine their own thinking about the issues, and in the process enlighten *them*. Those of us who have written editorials for a living, or who have had to organize arguments for debate, realize that there is no better way to come to grips with an issue than to put one's thoughts on paper, to muster arguments in carefully wrought sentences. This is not easy work. It requires some mental discipline. But it puts the mind in gear. It drives the laboring writer to an understanding of the subject and his own relation to it that he can acquire in no other way. Reading what someone else has written can't do that. Therefore, to the remedies offered by Charles Rembar, let me add this one: When a speech writer provides a candidate with a particularly lucid discussion of any issue, we should find out who that writer is, and elect *him* or *her*.

It would be nice to think that Hubert Humphrey lost his bid for the presidency because the voters wanted to hear more than just a few words of his own. But the depressing fact is that Humphrey's opponent was reading other people's speeches, too. And as long as the press and the public don't strenuously object, that is not likely to change.

QUESTION: Your message is very clear, but aside from the demand or lack of it on the part of the public for opinion, from a practical standpoint it is very difficult for me to see how the politician actively engaged in trying to carry out his work as a manager or as a candidate can have time to write. I grew up in a discipline of having to put ideas on paper, and it takes a terribly long time. If our candidates and our governing people were to spend the time they would have to to meaningfully put their ideas on the paper, how could they do their job in carrying out their function as either a candidate or as a governor?

MR. HAMILTON: That is *the* question. You have proposed a correct question: Is it a matter of time? Having never been a politician, I am in no position to answer that. But I believe that some of the busiest of our leaders do the most writing. I have a friend who was for 18 months a speech writer for Senator Frank Church, who was himself a good writer, a brilliant orator, and a very busy senator, chairman of the Foreign Relations Committee, and a man of great energy as well as great intellect. Yet I was told by my friend that Church wrote probably 90 percent of his own speeches and other public statements. The speech writer's job in Church's office was to go in and sit in front of his desk with a pad and pencil and take notes as Church said what he wanted to say. He told him what he wanted said in his speech. The speech writer then went back to his office and made a draft which the senator would read over, touch up, and send back. The speech writer would make another draft, and Church would do much the same thing. So at the time the speech was finished and ready for delivery it was almost all by Senator Church. He did take a lot of time with his speeches even though they were partly the product of a speech writer.

I'm told by the same person that it was well known in the Capitol that the laziest, least effective members of Congress were the ones most inclined not to write their own stuff, who leaned most heavily on the words of speech writers. The impulse to say what you want to say effectively, in your own words, may be strong enough to require you to give up some other things in order to do it, or to find the time to do it even if it means putting in a long day. I have not, as I say, ever been in that position, so I don't know.

QUESTION: Didn't the presidential ghostwriting practice really start with Franklin Roosevelt using Harold Ickes and Harry Hopkins? I have an impression that before that, presidents probably wrote most of their own speeches.

MR. HAMILTON: I'd like to hear some other opinions on that because I don't know. Perhaps somebody here knows the history better than I do. I am aware that Ickes and Hopkins were indeed very active in that period.

COMMENT: They were quite notorious. We knew who they were.

MR. HAMILTON: We also knew that FDR himself was a pretty good speech writer, but I think you are right that he also relied rather heavily on others. I don't know before him how many did that. I don't know how far back you have to go to find a president who wrote his own stuff, probably quite a ways, I suppose.

COMMENT: Coolidge could have used a ghostwriter.

COMMENT: This is more of a comment than a question, but it seems to me our two leading candidates [Bush and Dukakis] as well as other politicians very studiously avoid saying anything rather than trying to get somebody else to put words in their mouths. I think this is quite wrong.

MR. HAMILTON: It certainly is. That's one reason I want to hear from the candidate in his own words because his own words will tell me whether he is fuzzy or being clear on a subject. In politics, as you all know, the purpose is to mislead, actually, and so a politician will speak in phrases deliberately designed to obscure rather than to clarify, and will say as little as he has to. And you are absolutely right. That's depressing to me, that the goal of a speech must be to cover up the issue rather than to disclose it.

QUESTION: Is speech writing an American phenomenon? I can't imagine a Churchill using a speech writer.

MR. HAMILTON: I can't either. I can't imagine that. I would hate to be writing a speech for Winston Churchill. I can't imagine anything more horrendous or punishing.

QUESTION: Do you think this ability to speak the language of men is something you are born with or is this something that you can get at least partly by training? Maybe the problem is that our politicians don't get the training that they once got.

MR. HAMILTON: I think that's true. The way we are educated makes a big difference. The leaders of the country, going back as far as Jefferson tended to be better-educated people. Jefferson was educated in the classics, with Greek and Latin—a brilliant man with a fine education. His father required that he be well educated, and I think that he was more typical than not of the Framers. We don't have that kind of education now. In addition to that, we also now have role models who get up on a public platform and instead of saying, "I hope that we will ratify this treaty before he goes to Moscow," say, "I would hope that he would ratify this treaty before he goes to Moscow." If those are to be our role models, we do not grow up with an impulse to talk clearly and effectively. So education surely has a lot to do with it as well as the milieu, the political environment in which we live, where it is the rule rather than the exception to speak in a fuzzy language.

QUESTION: Perhaps part of the problem is the instant reporting in speeches now; the leader would have to write so many different speeches. In the period before television, before widespread immediate reporting, he could give the same speech again and again without being noticed to the degree that it is noticed today.

MR. HAMILTON: I think the typical candidate does give the same speech. He has a set stump speech, and my impression is that that speech is the one he gives at every whistle-stop. He will elaborate on it from time to time, but they do give pretty much the same speech. The press simply does not cover all these speeches because it is not worth their while. So if you live in Podunk and you hear the candidate speak there, you may have the impression that he has given you an original piece of work, and just 40 miles down the road they will think the same thing.

COMMENT: And the language has been modified a little bit.

MR. HAMILTON: It might be modified a little bit to suit the locale. He has a staff along with him who will tell him what the people do here and what line would give a little local flavor to his speech.

QUESTION: Did Adlai Stevenson write his own speeches or did he just provide the style of delivery?

MR. HAMILTON: Adlai Stevenson, as I recall, had a speech writer who was underworked because Stevenson did write the bulk of his speeches. One report that I've seen said that he wrote 80 to 90 percent of his own stuff. And he was a marvelous writer; there was no point in him ever hiring anybody else to do his writing; he was a wonderful writer with a nice and leavening sense of humor.

QUESTION: Is there perhaps a decline in the art and practice of debate? It was brought to mind by the mention of Churchill. In the debates in the House of Commons, he wouldn't—at least in those days—get very far with canned speeches. You had to respond.

MR. HAMILTON: If I were the president of the University of Virginia, I would make debate a required subject, no matter what discipline you were in. I would require debate of everybody for graduation because debate is the finest tool for fashioning a good, lively mind and the ability to respond effectively on your feet. That requires the development of mental discipline, the ability to create a logical chain of ideas that are persuasive, and to do so fast on your feet. That ought to make you successful in politics. We don't require that.

Look at the debates we have on TV; they aren't anything that Churchill would recognize as a debate. They are interesting and fun to watch, but they don't strike me as the kind of debate that you hear in Harvard or on a debating team.

NARRATOR: Could we come back to the issue of time? We've all had our own experiences with people who worked in the private sector or in education and then went into government. Mine was with Dean Rusk. Dean Rusk used to ask staff for paragraphs. He'd say, "Write me a paragraph," but by the time he had put them in a speech or in a report, the paragraph you had written was almost unrecognizable because he crafted it in his own way and framed it in his own language. You were hard-pressed to see what you had given him in the final product.

Then he moved into government and testified hundreds of times regularly before committees of Congress. Vietnam came up and he was harassed and buffeted on that. He just didn't have time to write his own speeches. Yet here was a Rhodes scholar, a person who, if you've listened to the former secretaries of state, can still express himself as readily and easily as anyone we've had. But he couldn't get the time to do it.

Perhaps there is something about the organization of government and the way we use people. Dean Rusk has said if he had to do it over again he'd see fewer people. But even in a place like this, if you see fewer people you are always tormented by the fact that the ones you don't see may have been the most important for you, whether they are students or people who might join in what we are doing here. So you are driven in big and little jobs by all of this. Is there anything else that can be said about that question?

MR. HAMILTON: I'm sure there is. I think that in the case of Dean Rusk, it is probably very true that he simply lacked the time. Clearly he didn't lack the capacity or the ability, as you point out. He was certainly able to write his own speeches. But a great many of the politicians of today are spending their time on other things that I don't think are as important as communicating: ceremonial things and visitors to the Capitol. The way Congress runs, I think, may be partly to blame. Senator Daniel Evans of Washington State is leaving the Senate because he says he couldn't stand the frustration of trying to get anything done in that body. He said Congress is an impossible organ to move. He was accustomed to state government where the governor could get something done. He said a senator is helpless to get anything done. It is because of the way Congress organizes itself and the way it functions—too many subcommittees and committee meetings going on all the time. There is no way in the world to keep track of the legislation, no way in the world to effectively debate a bill, because there is nobody there to listen to him talk. They are all at committee meetings, having hearings on this and hearings on that, and perhaps a lot of that *is* important. But in Evans's view it took away from his primary job, which was to create legislation, so he is leaving. He'll be succeeded by a lesser man who will undoubtedly be able to get along in that environment. But to a really intelligent and ambitious person it didn't work. There was something wrong with the way Congress was organized. Evans, of course, isn't the only person who has complained about it.

NARRATOR: Before we came in you said something about staff as being part of the problem. Would you care to elaborate at all on that?

MR. HAMILTON: Well, I was just repeating what so many other observers are saying about Congress. The burgeoning of the staff has had the effect of separating the elected from the electors. Staff, as a filter, has become a very dense one. Staff does the work, staff knows this, staff knows that, staff knows where this is or that is, where this bill is or that bill is. And the elected person is run by the staff, and the staff is just too big. I am just saying what a lot of other people close to the scene are saying.

QUESTION: I was going to ask you about the remedy, if any, for this situation. Candidates, press, and public all seem to be willing to settle for this sort of inferior kind of communication. Do you propose a constitutional amendment?

MR. HAMILTON: Mr. Rembar proposed that, I didn't.

QUESTION: You said something very important regarding priorities. Just how much importance do you attach to speaking this language of men that you were talking about? If you let other things displace that as the highest priority, then you are going to get this situation. So I guess the remedy is to work somehow for a change in priorities, but can you be more specific?

MR. HAMILTON: I don't know how specific you could be. I suppose that one person's priorities would not necessarily be the same as another's, and shouldn't be. I may be a member of a very tiny minority which feels this way. But my own priority would be pretty clear to me; I want to know what kind of person I'm asked to elect to Congress or to the presidency, and I can't tell what kind of person he is. That's my highest priority. I don't care how good-looking he is or what a "great communicator" he is said to be. I don't think we have a great communicator [Reagan] in the White House right now. I would like to have one there, I really would. I want to be communicated with, and I want to be communicated with in somebody's words that tell me something about him or her, and I don't feel that I'm getting it. A lot of people are very much disturbed about that, so that may not be a minority view.

QUESTION: I have a question and then a comment. The question is: How frustrating is it to write for somebody else? The comment is, I remember reading that Kissinger asked one of his aides one time to write a speech on some subject. After about the third draft the gentleman who wrote the speech said, "Mr. Kissinger, this is the best I can do." Kissinger answered, "Thank you. In that event I'll read it then."

MR. HAMILTON: As to the question, the friend to whom I referred earlier who was a speech writer for Senator Church told me it was very frustrating to write for him, because he knew that what he was writing was not going to be read or printed. Church would rewrite it in his own style and by the time Church had finished with the speech writer's work, Church thought it was his own. One time my friend said that he'd written a speech for Church in which he had coined a phrase that he thought fell rather well on the ear. Church liked it well enough to include it in his speech. My friend then said, referring to the phrase, "That went over pretty well," and Church said, "Thank you."

QUESTION: Mr. Hamilton, aren't you making the assumption that oratorical ability and managerial or executive ability are necessarily correlated? Isn't there a possibility that the capacity for spontaneous oratory, such as we see in Reverend Mr. Jackson, may not be correlated with the kind of qualities which make for effective administration? I think, too, that the capacity for revision after revision, which you suggest was characteristic of Senator Church and which was characteristic of Governor Stevenson, may also be associated with a kind of perfectionism which makes decision making rather difficult. Stevenson at least was criticized for being so concerned with the ultimate outcome of a speech that it was difficult for him to make up his mind.

MR. HAMILTON: I think it is true that the two are not the same. A person can be an excellent manager and a poor speech writer. But if he is writing his own stuff, at least we have that part of him to judge. In the case of Jesse Jackson, we have that to judge him by. Also, as you are well aware, we are judging Jackson on the basis of what we assume to be his managerial ability or lack of it. In fact, the thing that is dogging him now is the perception that he has none and that the best he's got is an oratorical flourish. So as the campaign proceeds, people are judging him on both bases. What is his background in management? They find very little, but they are charmed by his oratory. His oratory has been very effective for him, but when it comes down to the wire I don't think he is going to make it, because of the perception that he is lacking in managerial ability. So we have to judge him on that angle, too.

QUESTION: On the other hand, as a newspaperman, would you have wanted to have listened to vintage Eisenhower through the 1952 and 1956 campaign?

MR. HAMILTON: We heard quite a bit of it at the press conferences, as you recall. I think if Ike had sat down and written out his own speeches, they would have been readable. On his feet he talked a kind of gibberish, but many of us would in that situation. People laughed at him; reporters laughed at Ike because he seemed so unintelligible in his press conferences. He was ungrammatical and had a hard time expressing himself on his feet. But I would be satisfied; I don't require the guy being brilliant on his feet if he can sit down and dash off something with a pencil and make it readable. His own words—thoughtful words—are important.

NARRATOR: The Eisenhower case raises the question whether what we get in politics, given all the constraints, the milieu, and the setting, is the real person, because Eisenhower in a small group was absolutely captivating. I was present at a working luncheon for about 20 people on the 55th floor of the RCA Building one time. A famous scientist, Warren Weaver, said at the end, "Eighty percent of you in this room are Democrats, but at the end of this discussion if Ike had said, 'Go to the window and jump out,' I'll bet 50 or 60 percent of you would have done it." He absolutely swayed that group. On another occasion half the people snickered at what was supposed to be an off-the-cuff speech, but pretty soon you could hear a pin drop, he was so captivating.

In the military and political arenas are there so many things we are afraid of saying? Are we so worried that what we say will get us into trouble that even the current chairman of the Joint Chiefs, with a Ph.D. in political science, begins to hedge when he moves into sensitive areas? Most of what he says is a textbook case in clarity. But it's these two areas, politics and the military, that are so fraught with consequences if you say the wrong thing, that even an Eisenhower, with an absolutely contagious quality of exciting you and bringing you into his milieu, can't really let it out the way they do in more private groups. Do military people talk about what you can and can't say?

GENERAL WHITLATCH: Endlessly. I think that in the military and other segments of government, where people are exposed to thousands of tidbits of information that are classified and millions of tidbits that are unclassified, after a while you become very hesitant to say anything because you can't remember on which side the item fell. But I would think that there is a duplicate problem. That's when someone like Admiral Crowe, trying to speak or answer a question at a press conference, is also faced with the problem of making sure he doesn't say something that's contradictory to what might have been said over in the White House. In this particular administration that's a significant problem. I don't think the military is unique. There is a continuing problem of being hesitant to say something that borders on the classified, and still being intelligible when you respond to a question.

NARRATOR: I remember something Eisenhower once told his press secretary, James Hagerty, before a press conference. When Hagerty said, "Aren't you worried about how you are going to answer this?", Eisenhower said, "No, I'll just confuse them."

MR. HAMILTON: Eisenhower was a delightful person—you are right about that—and the country loved him. In fact there is quite a similarity between the effect of Eisenhower and the effect of Reagan on the public; you know: "I like Ike" and they love Reagan. That part of it seems to have little to do with their ability to communicate orally, effectively. Ike didn't have it, Reagan has to depend on others, yet by the sheer force of personality they have achieved quite a linkage with the public.

NARRATOR; I'm sure I speak for all of you in thanking Mr. and Mrs. Ladd Hamilton for stopping off on their long trip east, and we hope it won't be long before they come back again. We hope you continue to challenge and stimulate us with your very thoughtful and lucid writing. Thank you very much.

CHAPTER 11

Presidential Rhetoric, Humor, and Social Criticism

RUSSELL BAKER

NARRATOR: Russell Baker hardly needs any introduction. He was born in Virginia and now lives in Leesburg, where, thanks to the miracle of electronic communication, he does most of his writing. He is the only American to have won the Pulitzer Prize both in literature, for his biography *Growing Up*, and in journalism. His career certainly demonstrates a devotion to the printed word. He has published a stream of memorable works: *American in Washington*, 1961; *No Cause for Panic*, 1964; *All Things Considered*, 1965; *Our Next President*, 1968; *Poor Russell's Almanac*, 1972; *The Upside Down Man*, 1977; *So This Is Depravity*, written with others, 1980; *Home Again, Home Again*, 1979; and *Growing Up*, 1982. He has been the recipient of the Frank Sullivan Memorial Award, the George Polk Award, the Pulitzer Prize—twice, as I mentioned—and the Elmer Holmes Bobst prize for nonfiction.

He received his degree from Johns Hopkins. He has had an office in New York but has done his writing in such far-flung places as Massachusetts and Leesburg. We had hoped that with our interest in the presidency and rhetoric and his interest in that subject, we could have some conversation on them, but we will likely go well beyond that topic.

Sander Vanocur, a close friend, has said that Russell Baker is the foremost creative mind in social commentary in America. Perhaps that's the best way to introduce him to all of you.

MR. BAKER: Thank you, Ken. I'd like to have Sander Vanocur eulogize me at my funeral. You made a good start. I seem to have gone through life collecting plaques, but believe me it doesn't feel that way to me. I'd like to apologize to the people sitting out in the bleachers there. I'm sorry you won't have the agreeable spectacle of watching me as I grope for words, twitching, scratching my head, and chewing my cud. That's often the whole sport of the event. I'd really like to have you all do the talking and ask me what interests you. I am prepared to answer any number of questions.

I once went to a press conference given by President de Gaulle. One received an engraved invitation to these events. We went up to the Elysée Palace and entered a magnificent room decked with Baccarat crystal, lovely chairs; it was an impressive setting. When we were assembled there, perhaps 500 of us, the general himself came in, followed by his entire Cabinet, who then sat over on the side of the room looking not at the press but at him. He stood up, looking very de Gaullesque, and said, "Are there any questions?" The man down front said, "Yes, *mon general*, I have a question," and he asked his question, and de Gaulle nodded and said, "Are there any more questions?" And he went around the room and took questions from everybody. When the questions were exhausted, he then prepared to answer, and he made a speech that lasted 45 minutes in which so far as I could make out he didn't answer more than two questions that had been asked.

It occurred to me later that de Gaulle, when he came into the room, was really saying that he had a lot of answers and wanted to know if there were any questions that fit the answers that he had. I have a lot of answers, and if you have any questions I'd be delighted to try to give you some.

As for presidents, I have spent a lot of time covering the men. They were all men, regrettably, who either wanted to be president, were presidents, or became presidents. I came to Washington in the 1950s to cover the White House. I covered General Eisenhower. I subsequently went out and covered the Senate, which was full of presidential timber—as we always call it for some reason that escapes me—full of knot heads. There was Jack Kennedy, who sat in the back row, and Bobby Kennedy, who was the chief counsel to the so-called McClellan Committee, which had been Joe McCarthy's old committee. Lyndon Johnson was down front as majority leader; Nixon was presiding as vice president. Barry Goldwater was out on the far right on the Republican side, grousing about Eisenhower's "dime store New Deal"; Hubert Humphrey was back in the middle, talking, talking, talking. Senator Russell, who had run for president and had been very embittered by the experience, was down front whispering to Lyndon Johnson, telling him how to run things. Stuart Symington, who looked so much like a president that it was a pity he never became one, but who was everybody's second choice in 1960, was there. It's a long list.

Covering these men, I was struck with the unstartling fact of their humanity, how ordinary they were for the most part. I would make an exception of Lyndon Johnson, who was extraordinary. But for the most part they were the most ordinary kind of men imaginable to somebody like myself who was a kid and had come into this business completely innocent, with a conventional high-school history-book view of presidents as mortal statues. It was dispiriting to discover that these were the same kind of people I'd known since I was a kid but that they had grown up. I could see them as overgrown boys. I could imagine what they'd been like as young men, as that awful "big man on campus" back in high school who ran the prom. You could see where they had all come from. It was very disillusioning to me as a journalist, and I said, "I've got to find another line of work." But I couldn't do anything but journalism, of course. So I had to find a line of work in journalism that was more gratifying to me than that, and this is what I found: sitting here at the University of Virginia, talking to poor people out there who can't even see and who are sitting there very patiently instead of stomping their feet. Now I'd prefer we go to questions.

QUESTION: What do you think of Garrison Keillor?

MR. BAKER: I love Garrison Keillor. He did a reading of my book *Growing Up* for Minnesota public radio. He read about three-quarters of it in about eight hours of tape. He read it better than I could have read it. Keillor is a natural storyteller, I think. It is an unusual kind of thing for our culture to have produced a storyteller, somebody who works in words for the ear, because the whole thrust of our society is so intensely aimed toward gratifying the eye that people don't really listen any more. You've noticed that in conversations. You are having a conversation with somebody, and you become aware very quickly he is not listening; he is just waiting for you to shut up so he can talk. This is inevitable, I suppose, in this kind of society. And here Keillor has done this marvelous thing. He has made the whole country listen for 20 to 30 minutes while he tells these really quite ordinary stories about ordinary people. It's a gift, a blessing.

QUESTION: It seems to me that the press, the so-called "liberal" press, became pussycats and just sat in the lap of the Reagan administration beginning in 1980. Your colleague R. W. Apple was here and said that one of the reasons for this was that there was too much socializing between the press and the administration. I would go on to say that the only people who weren't pussycats were people like you and Art Buchwald, humorists who went ahead and dug at the administration all they cared to do. What happened?

MR. BAKER: I won't speak for Buchwald, but I think I've tried to be equally unfair to all administrations. I found the Reagan administration very hard to deal with because it was as though nobody was listening. It was like shouting down a rain barrel, and after a while I tended to give it up and let it go. Everybody liked Reagan; everybody knew that he was not on top of the job; everybody accepted the criticisms of him that were made by, as you call it, the "liberal" press, and the attitude was, so what? Everything was going along fine, and you got tired when you got no response.

It was wonderful to write about Lyndon Johnson. For one thing, you didn't have to invent anything. If you were in the humor business, you just reported what Johnson had done, and then Johnson would get furious. He'd strike you off lists: no more invitations to dance at the White House. You were really getting results. And people cared.

If you wrote about Nixon—oh, Nixon, he was a case. People loved Nixon. Not a lot of people loved Nixon, but the people who loved Nixon loved him with a passion. When you said something that made fun of Nixon, the mail was full of hate. You either loved Nixon or you hated him, I guess.

Reagan was not a political figure, in a way. He was the grand old man, and America has now put him behind and pressed him in the family Bible, like an old rose, I think, and gone on to the next thing.

Ben Bradlee of the *Washington Post* once told me that they had made an assiduous effort in the first year or two of the administration to correct Reagan. You know, Reagan sort of made things up as he went along; he often got them wrong, and often they hadn't happened at all. The *Post* would regularly run little features correcting what the President had said yesterday. And Bradlee said, "Nobody cared." Finally, they got no reaction at all. Reagan was inventing the truth, as it were. In a way, it turned out to be a remarkable administration. He ended the Cold War.

QUESTION: Did he really help?

MR. BAKER: It is my opinion that the Cold War is over. It happened on Reagan's watch, and he must get the credit for it.

QUESTION: Did you like covering Eisenhower, and what was Mamie like?

MR. BAKER: No, it was a very tough White House to cover. It was really sealed up. You couldn't get any information, except what was issued by the press secretary. You never saw Mamie, except getting on and off airplanes. There wasn't a lot of information that came out of the Eisenhower administration that they didn't want issued. You felt that you were totally manipulated by the public relations people in that presidency.

QUESTION: I'm curious about what was so extraordinary about Lyndon Johnson.

MR. BAKER: Everything about him was extraordinary. Of all those men whom I've covered since I came to Washington, Lyndon Johnson is the only real biography. The rest are a magazine article at best. In 3,500 words you can dispose of most of them. But you could write and write and write and write about Johnson, and you still don't begin to have him.

COMMENT: Is Johnson too slippery?

MR. BAKER: No, he's complex; he is interesting. His humanity is all up there for you to see. He is everything, and just when you think you've got him, suddenly you discover something else that makes everything you've learned wrong. You never know who he is going to be at any minute. He is a fascinating character.

QUESTION: Mr. Baker, you have written such delightful, humorous articles. Occasionally you have also written some superb articles that took the high moral ground. I was wondering why you didn't do more of that.

MR. BAKER: Well, there are basically three kinds of columns: one is the inside guy who is giving you whispers; another is the analyst who looks at complicated situations and tries to unthread them for you; and the third is a moralist. All humorists—people who work in humor forms, like myself—are moralists. You are constantly gilding the philosophic pill. Once in a while I will, instead of trying to present the argument in an interesting way which people tend to think is funny—it's just a way of engaging their attention—I'm too lazy or too tired that day, and so I'll just write out what I really think. People say, "That's great. You were serious today. Why aren't you serious more often?" The fact is I'm always serious. It's just a question of how you approach the material. Just because sometimes I approach it in a way that may seem to the reader to be lighthearted doesn't mean that what I am saying is not very serious.

To answer your question specifically, until recently I've written three columns a week. If you do three columns a week displaying your own moral superiority, you wear out your welcome pretty quickly.

QUESTION: Mr. Baker, do you mind commenting on first ladies? Which one did you enjoy covering the most?

MR. BAKER: I never comment on first ladies because I don't think they ask for it in most cases. I am kind of old-fashioned. I was raised by a very stern mother according to old sexist principles which have it that gentlemen don't abuse ladies. I know some of you will hate those terms, but I'm sorry, that's in my genes, my marrow. I can't bring myself to deal honestly with people who really got themselves into this awful predicament because of the ambition or foolishness of their husbands.

I think Nancy Reagan, more than any other, was glad to be there, and she was quite active, as a matter of fact. She is the only one I can think of offhand.

QUESTION: Did Rosalynn Carter regret it?

MR. BAKER: I always forget the Carter presidency. I did write one or two pieces about Nancy Reagan, I think, when she bought the china, the famously, outrageously priced china. Even then, that's not my business to abuse women who are in unfortunate predicaments, and I just haven't done it.

QUESTION: You spoke of feeling as if you were shouting down a rain barrel during the Reagan years. Did the letters that you got reflect something that made you want to try some other subject, or were there not enough letters? What was your reaction at the time?

MR. BAKER: I should say that I don't judge response by mail. I think if you start judging your response by the mail flow, it is a terrible mistake. If I want to get heavy mail all I have to do is write a column on behalf of gun control, and they'll bring it in by the barrel; the same goes for advocating higher taxes. I don't judge it that way. There is a way you can sense who is reading what, but I'm not quite sure of it.

I first noticed in the Carter years that whenever I wrote about Carter, I could hear my readers turning to the next page the minute I said "Carter." I think that went on into Reagan. (It is vulgar people like me who now find it fashionable to make fun of Carter, who I think in some ways was a very good President.) There was the beginning of a falling off of interest in presidents in the Carter years, some kind of reaction against presidential copy. Presidents somehow began to cease to be good copy. Reagan was good copy because he wasn't really a president, if you think about it. You know, it was like having a star; he was a star. Now we've got Bush. You begin to see the same thing about Bush that we saw about Carter. He's not very good copy; he is not a star.

To go back to the readers, how do you know you're losing them? I don't know how you know it, but you can tell from what people say around the office. If you find that people around the office aren't reading you, you know you are in trouble. I noticed in the Carter years I wouldn't get any reaction on Carter pieces from people around the office. It occurred to me people weren't reading about Carter, and I began writing less about Carter because, after all, I am a commercial writer, and I'm interested in holding an audience. Every columnist's nightmare is the day when everybody who buys the paper looks at his column and says "Why do they keep printing this old guy?" and turns the page. You are always sensitive to that.

QUESTION: What impact can humor have on the political process, especially regarding presidents?

MR. BAKER: It is almost impossible to quantify when you start talking about the impact of humor. My memory goes back to Adlai Stevenson, who was at the time considered a great wit, a funny man in some ways. That was one of the things said of Stevenson, and when people talked about why he was beaten so easily by Eisenhower, Stevenson's humor was one of the things constantly cited. He made jokes, and General Eisenhower didn't make jokes. That's nonsense, of course. General Eisenhower could have beaten anybody who ran those years. But humor was always cited against Stevenson, and for that reason politicians in the 1950s were very cautious about telling jokes. There was really no humor to speak of in public life until Kennedy was elected in 1961, and then it exploded.

Taking it from the other side, we have Gerald Ford, a president who was in some ways almost destroyed by bad jokes about him. The impersonation of Ford by Chevy Chase on "Saturday Night Live"–falling down, bumping his head, sticking the telephone in his mouth or whatever—tended to make Ford look absurd in a gross way that I think was probably damaging.

You couldn't make a joke about Reagan. He loved it; he loved jokes on himself. His equanimity was indestructible.

It was fun to make fun of Kennedy because you felt he was tougher than you were. He would always give it back to you. He could hurt you more than you could hurt him.

Nixon was a humorless man, and you always felt you were hurting Nixon, that a joke or any humor applied to Nixon hurt him so that he couldn't respond to it. He had no defense against it, and it was truly painful to him. He just made another mark against your name in his book. I don't think Nixon was ever politically vulnerable to humor; I don't think he was hurt in the least by it.

QUESTION: Do you feel that the current jokes about Vice President Quayle are really having an impact on him and on his potential as a president if something should happen to Bush?

MR. BAKER: I don't know. I'd have to ask you all that, but I would think the public picture of him that has been conveyed since the campaign would not promote his chances of getting a nomination for the presidency in 1996. I should think it would even raise the question if there is a second term of whether Bush could somehow get rid of him gracefully. I suppose humor has been one of the things that has helped to create that image, but before there was any humor in the Quayle situation there was Quayle himself. There were the facts: Quayle's National Guard problem, his law school problems, and Quayle. There is nothing funny about the facts; they just sat out there, and the Bush campaign fought back against them rather cleverly. But once that was all settled what happened was that the facts were set in the public mind, as it were, and that was material for nightclub comics to start to work on. But the facts came first, the humorous exploitation later.

On the other hand, if you look at Jerry Ford, what did he ever do? Did he fall down once or bump his head going through a door? From that came the fictional notion that he was a graceless oaf. In fact Ford was perhaps one of the most physically graceful men I have ever seen in public office. He was a natural athlete, a big man who "moved well," as they say in the theater. Somehow he became the victim of this burlesque humor to the effect that he was an oaf.

QUESTION: How would one compare politicians as humorists? Stevenson may have been unusual in that he made fun of himself. Maybe Reagan does that. You haven't mentioned Gene McCarthy; he is a kind of humorist. Now some people see Robert Dole as having a certain gift as a humorist.

MR. BAKER: Stevenson was different from McCarthy and Dole. Stevenson's humor was a good-natured, warm humor; it was good humor. It spoke of a good-humored man. When he was confronted with a situation, he tended to smile and look at the bright side of it for a moment. It was not altogether self-deprecatory. I recall some of his comments aimed at the Republican party in the 1952 campaign—the difficulties of hauling them, kicking and screaming, into the 20th century. He had a quick wit, but it was good-natured humor, not a mean humor. People always say "Why can't you be like Will Rogers? He never met a man he didn't like." I always say, "Well, Will Rogers never left the house." Adlai Stevenson's humor was that sort.

I was covering a campaign down in Florida somewhere, and we were on a university campus there, maybe in Tallahassee. The students wanted to give Stevenson a donkey, so they found this enormous jackass—it must have been eight feet high. They brought it out behind him, but he wasn't aware it was there. He was talking into the microphone, and somebody tapped him and said, "Governor, we have something to give you," and he turned and looked at this thing and recoiled. He immediately said, "I've been given sundry donkeys in my time, but this is the first I ever had which is big enough to kick an elephant to death." He could do that right off the top of his head.

Gene McCarthy and Dole, of course, are supposed to be mean spirited. Bob Dole is "mean"—"mean Bob." If anybody has a right to be mean, I guess it is Bob Dole. But it's Will Roger's humor that gets you elected.

Eugene McCarthy is subtle. He is a classic Catholic intellectual. The best example of his brand of humor came when he used to call me up once in a while and suggest a column to me. His ideas were such that the punch line would have had to be in Latin.

I'm sure somebody has told the great McCarthy story about the year George Romney was running and McCarthy was campaigning. It was 1968, and Romney made the news that day by announcing that he was going to come out against the war in Vietnam. He had been a hawk previously, and he explained that to the press by saying he had been brainwashed. Well, this was a big item on the Associated Press that day, and McCarthy was plane-hopping small towns in New Hampshire. McCarthy's press secretary tore it off the wire, got on the plane with him, and gave it to him. The press secretary, Seymour Hirsch, told me this story. He said that he told McCarthy, "When we get to the next stop, the press is going to ask if you have any comment on this Romney brainwashing statement. Whatever you do, say 'no comment,'" and McCarthy nodded. They got on the plane and flew awhile, and he could see McCarthy thinking, and he knew he was going to do something awful when they got off. Indeed, they got off, and here came the press, the thundering herd, saying, "Senator, Governor Romney has just said he has been brainwashed. Do you have any comment?" McCarthy said, "I always thought in Romney's case a light rinse would do." Now that's a very funny line, but at the time people tended to say, "He ought to be on television instead of in the White House."

QUESTION: Why do you think Dole has a right to be mean?

MR. BAKER: He has a right because of his war injuries and the immense physical pain that he suffered. What he must have had to do to make his body perform the things that it does again could only have been done by somebody with really an overpowering sense of irony, which leads to a kind of embittering humor, and yet it's a form of survival. His is the humor of a survivor, I think. He has been all the way to the end, looked down, and come back.

COMMENT: He hurts himself at times with his humor.

MR. BAKER: Yes, but it has helped him to live too and to get where he is. It must embitter him more to realize that he can't get there because of it. Bush hasn't been through that.

QUESTION: Would you say, Mr. Baker, that candidates themselves ought to stay away from either sharp political humor or the wonderfully funny, whimsical humor of Adlai Stevenson?

MR. BAKER: Yes, I think candidates certainly should leave humor alone these days. You never know how it is going to explode. As a matter of fact, candidates these days leave almost everything alone. Making statements about policy certainly is left alone.

As far as I can make out, the George Bush we elected in the campaign was invented by two or three people, Roger Ailes's images and Peggy Noonan's words and so on. I'd never seen this George Bush before. He was pledging allegiance to the flag, doing all those strange things, and denouncing the American Civil Liberties Union. George Bush was that rare thing in American politics, a complete gentleman. But he put himself in the hands of people who were going to get him elected, and he turned into a Mr. Hyde figure to get elected.

The day after the campaign, he was George Bush again. I listened to his first press conference the day after the election, and that guy we had voted for had just disappeared. Here was good old George back. He was being pleasant to people; he was not saluting the flag; it was as though Willie Horton had never existed. It was like Dorothy coming back from Oz. There is no place like home; there is nothing like being the real George Bush again.

I should think most people running for high office these days would look at that Bush campaign and take caution against doing anything that is spontaneous. If you want to get elected, I would say you better call in the professionals and do what they tell you.

NARRATOR: Dean Acheson and Dean Rusk used to complain that Walter Lippmann would never have written some of his columns if he'd come to see them and talk with them about it. In organizing a column, does the journalist have any responsibility to go to the public official and include him or her among the sources?

MR. BAKER: I don't think so, particularly if you write a column like Walter Lippmann's. Lippmann considered himself the equal of a secretary of state, didn't he? I didn't know Lippmann well. Lippmann liked to talk to everybody, but the talk was of a social nature. He liked to see people at dinner and have long, rambling conversations, but he was not a reporter like Scotty Reston, for example, who when the question troubled him he'd get on the phone and call Dean Acheson. I must say in that regard, considering what you are attributing to Acheson, that Acheson would never answer the phone when Scotty called him up for this kind of information.

I wouldn't think to call about an opinion piece. I never deal with facts; if I have a fact I'm in trouble. I don't write that kind of column, but of reporters who do, I think most of them wouldn't bother to call because they'd assume that the person they are calling will only try to use them even if he answers the phone, and he probably wouldn't answer the phone. That would be my surmise, but I've never written that kind of column and have no urge to. I'm glad I don't have to deal with that sort of philosophical problem.

QUESTION: On the other side of that, you mentioned that Gene McCarthy had called you about a column he would like you to write. Is that something that happens very often, and how do you respond to them? How do others in your field respond?

MR. BAKER: That doesn't happen in my case, no. Politicians practically never call me, for obvious reasons. I have a reputation for being a humorist. I don't know why, but once you get that reputation you are considered dangerous, and the best thing you can do if you are a politician is to stay away. I think they feel it's like fooling around with rattlesnakes.

Gene McCarthy was different for whatever reason. He is one of the few politicians I ever made the mistake of cultivating personally, and it is a terrible mistake for a journalist to have a personal relationship with a politician. I made that mistake with McCarthy. One of the less evil results was that he called me once in a while with a suggestion for a humorous column, but I never took his suggestions.

QUESTION: Would a personal relationship inhibit you from writing objectively?

MR. BAKER: Yes, you can't very well eat somebody's food and then go back and tear him up in print, can you? That's one of the problems of working in Washington; so many reporters and columnists feel they have to run a soiree to get ahead there. It's not necessary in Washington, but it's fun;

their wives like it, and it inflates the ego to eat around with this year's people. It is something you just have to watch out for. It's bad business.

QUESTION: You mentioned twice that you feel you are putting people to sleep at this point. Who do you think is doing what you do? Who will do what you do so well when you decide to stop?

MR. BAKER: Well, I really don't know what I do sometimes, but it's the kind of column that is pretty good to do at the *New York Times*. The *Times* is an intensely competitive thing. It is like an ad agency in the old days, or *Time* magazine, and I'm the only guy in the paper whose job nobody else wants. I'm friends with everybody, and I assume that means that nobody else will do this job after I get rid of it. I really don't know what I'm doing that's so oddball. I'm just trying to write well about issues that everybody else is writing about. Does it need to be done? No, nothing *needs* to be done.

We used to think we needed competition in newspapers. Well, we discovered we don't. Newspapers just aren't competitive anymore. We are not very competitive in New York. We used to think we had to be competitive, but actually we put out a pretty good newspaper without competition, maybe better than we could with competition. But we also lose a kind of edge. We've lost something because of the lack of competition, but we've gained something also.

QUESTION: Why aren't there women humorists?

MR. BAKER: I had some shtick on this I used to do when I was on the lecture circuit. I would say, "There are no women humorists because to be a humorist you have to get beat up a lot when you are a kid on the way to school, and you have to have an unhappy childhood or a tragedy at a very early age." This developed the theme that there were no women humorists because nobody beat up little girls on the way to school. Well, that didn't work. Of course, now they beat up little girls, too. It is very modern to beat up little girls. You can't call them "ladies" any more. As a result, we have a lot of women humorists. It is really quite a good age for female humorists: Lily Tomlin is about the funniest performer around.

COMMENT: I enjoy Erma Bombeck. I think she's funny.

MR. BAKER: Erma Bombeck is a good example, yes. There are women working in this field.

QUESTION: What about Ellen Goodman? Sometimes she is quite funny and very serious.

MR. BAKER: She can be. She is more like me. She is not really a humorist; she is a preacher who is trying to gild the pill.

COMMENT: I suspect that the secret of the success of both you and Mark Russell is that you simply tell the truth.

MR. BAKER: You said that; I didn't. I would hate to have that lodged as a charge against me. One of the great conceits of newspapermen is that they are telling the truth by compiling facts. They live under the happy illusion that if you compile sufficient facts, you will produce the truth. You know, the truth has nothing to do with facts, does it? Truth is subjective invention once you get out of the laboratory. But newspapermen really believe they are telling the truth.

I used to believe it when I was a reporter. I'd go out and work hard, and I'd come back, and I'd get it *right* and print it. A couple of years later the memoirs would come along, the people who were involved, and I had it all wrong. It seemed true, but I didn't know 98 percent of what was happening. Everything was wrong. It left me very disillusioned with the pursuit of truth, and I would prefer that you not accuse me of doing that.

QUESTION: Speaking of truth and predicaments, how about Ollie North?

MR. BAKER: Why do you call him "Ollie"? I'm curious by the way everyone calls this man "Ollie."

COMMENT: Because of the newspapers.

MR. BAKER: Ollie North. I don't know; I feel he is a fall guy, myself. If I were on the jury, I'd say, "Oh, well, sure he did all these things; let's get him, but only after Reagan does his turn." At least under Nixon they sent Mitchell, Haldeman, and Ehrlichman to jail; everybody went to jail except the big man himself. I can understand you don't want to send the President to jail. I'm against that, but there are a lot of people between North and Reagan that are eligible for the calaboose.

What really puzzles me is why everybody calls him "Ollie." There are people in Washington who get called by their first name, and it is done by the press. It's one of the more unattractive aspects of the Washington press. For a long while nobody in Washington could write about Henry Kissinger without calling him "Henry." Here was this rather formidable man who many thought was rather an unpleasant and unsociable fellow, but to suggest, probably misleadingly, that you and he had breakfast every morning, it was "Henry this" and "Henry that." This is a terrible conceit that you get in the upper reaches of Washington journalism, and I think that's where "Ollie" came from.

COMMENT: We talk about "Jim" Wright and "Bob" Dole.

MR. BAKER: Jim and Bob. Jimbob. Another interesting thing in this same vein is the spread of nicknames. We had

Jimmy Carter; he wanted to be "Jimmy." Most of you know Tom Wicker. Tom had a terrible fight with the *Times* when he first came, because he didn't want to be "Thomas Wicker" in his byline; he wanted to be "Tom." The *Times* had never let anybody use a nickname in a by-line, and I think it was a mistake to let Tom do it. He should have been "Thomas Wicker." Surely the presidents' names ought not to be changed: Richard Nixon, not Dick. It's a kind of diction; you are patting yourself on the back. It's "Henry," "Dick Nixon told me," "Ollie North." It's a kind of thing no self-respecting newspaperman should do, and yet we all do it.

COMMENT: There's a spread of this on television; everybody who comes on a television show is on a first-name basis with the interviewer. I can remember being stunned when George McGovern said, "No, Mr. Rather." The idea of calling Dan Rather "Mr. Rather" on his television show was a novelty.

MR. BAKER: You must do it. I was recently on the "Today Show." I was trying to sell a book, one of the many disgraces that you submit to. I said to myself, "Bryant Gumbel is going to introduce me. Well, I'm not going to call him Bryant. I'm going to say 'Mr. Gumbel.'" I go on, and he asked the first question, and I said, "Well, Bryant." It goes with that territory.

QUESTION: What did you mean in saying that newspapers don't need competition?

MR. BAKER: I didn't say they didn't need it; I said that they can function well without it. There is a trade-off involved. With competition you tend to do certain things better than you do when there is no competition. You may even report more stories that otherwise you don't bother with. I think competition in the newspaper field tends to assure a broader area of coverage. On the other hand, competition can also make for very shabby coverage. The classic example of that was the Boston press, which as recently as the 1950s, maybe the 1960s, had seven or eight newspapers every morning, all famous for being absolutely terrible; because of the necessity of getting everything in, they simply could not afford to do it well.

What's happened with us at the *Times* since we've lost the competition is that we may be a bit smug about leaving things out. We don't have the *Herald Tribune* there with a story in the first edition that our editors see and say, "We've got to have that story," and then they get somebody out of bed, and we've extended the coverage. We don't have that any more, but the stories that we do have are done much better now than they used to be because we have time. We don't have to do them over the phone in the night. A reporter may work several days, even a couple of weeks on a story. They are better written because there is more time for that.

It is a trade-off, and I don't know how to balance it out. Some people say that television is the competition, but I don't see much competition from television. It's a headline service; that's about all. When the newspapers shut down, television doesn't know what to do. They have so few reporters.

QUESTION: What do you think of all this hoopla about ethics that's going on in Washington now?

MR. BAKER: I thought you were going to ask me about whether newspapermen should reveal their speaking fees. I was going to say I will not reveal mine here today.

QUESTION: Is it overblown?

MR. BAKER: I think it is overblown, yes. I assume and hope that it will pass over. However, a little more ethical concern than we have had in the past ten years or so wouldn't hurt, I think. I tend to be relaxed on this. Somewhere—I can't find the exact quote—H. L. Mencken once wrote that he'd hate to live in a society where you couldn't get a traffic ticket fixed because that wouldn't be a democracy. Somehow I find that strikes a great chord with me. Still, some of the ethical lapses have been egregious.

COMMENT: I'm sure a lot of people share my hope that you will conduct an old-fashioned school with disciples to preserve your kind of humor. I urge you to open a kind of a school of your own and collect disciples.

MR. BAKER: Are you suggesting another center at the University of Virginia?

NARRATOR: You can have half of this one.

MR. BAKER: It would be a very agreeable prospect, I assure you.

NARRATOR: With that tribute we will bring this part of the program to an end. We've tried for a long time to persuade Russell Baker he should come here, and we are certain that whatever the truth is, we were right in inviting him.